DAY HIKES AROUND

Bozeman

MONTANA

INCLUDING THE GALLATIN CANYON AND PARADISE VALLEY

Robert Stone

3rd EDITION

Day Hike Books, Inc.

RED LODGE, MONTANA

Published by Day Hike Books, Inc.
P.O. Box 865
Red Lodge, Montana 59068

Distributed by The Globe Pequot Press
246 Goose Lane
P.O. Box 480
Guilford, CT 06437-0480
800-243-0495 (direct order) · 800-820-2329 (fax order)
www.globe-pequot.com

Photographs by Robert Stone
Design by Paula Doherty

The author has made every attempt to provide accurate information in this book. However, trail routes and features may change—please use common sense and forethought, and be mindful of your own capabilities. Let this book guide you, but be aware that each hiker assumes responsibility for their own safety. The author and publisher do not assume any responsibility for loss, damage, or injury caused through the use of this book.

Cover photo:
Hyalite Lake from Hyalite Creek Trail, Hike 46

Back cover photo:
South Fork Trail to Pioneer Falls, Hike 48

Acknowledgements

*I wish to thank
Ted Lange at the Gallatin Valley Land Trust
for his assistance and dedication to the
expanding trail system in Bozeman.*

*I also wish to thank
Bill Olson for his hard work and devotion
in the development of the Big Sky
trail system.*

Table of Contents

THE HIKES

West Bridger Mountains

East Bridger Mountains · Bangtail Mountains

Bozeman Area

Hyalite Canyon

Madison River

Gallatin Canyon:
Gallatin Gateway to Big Sky

Yellowstone National Park
from the Gallatin

Paradise Valley:
Livingston to Gardiner

Regional Maps:

Suggested commercial maps for additional hiking:

U.S. Geological Survey topographic maps

U.S. Forest Service: Gallatin National Forest (East and West)

Beartooth Publishing: Bozeman–Big Sky–West Yellowstone

Crystal Bench Maps: Bozeman

Rocky Mountain Surveys: Spanish Peaks

Hiking Bozeman
Overview of the Hikes

Bozeman, Montana is an active, thriving town dating back to the 1880s. It is rich in character, history, and landscape. There are eight historical districts, a wide variety of museums, art galleries, musical events, and is home to Montana State University. Surrounded by extraordinary wilderness, Bozeman is also a gateway city to the Gallatin National Forest and Yellowstone National Park.

The Gallatin National Forest, part of the Greater Yellowstone Area, encompasses 1.8 million acres and contains some of the highest mountains in Montana. Six mountain ranges run through the national forest land—the Absaroka, Beartooth, Bridger, Crazy, Gallatin, and Madison Ranges. Many peaks rise above 10,000 feet. The sheer grandeur of this national forest includes the protected 259,000-acre Lee Metcalf Wilderness and the 945,000-acre Absaroka-Beartooth Wilderness. The forest also contains the headwaters to the Boulder, Gallatin, and Madison Rivers, plus hundreds of miles of creeks and tributaries. (Many of the rivers have a blue-ribbon rating for fishing.) The Gallatin National Forest has an abundance of wildlife, including black and grizzly bear, moose, elk, mountain lions, big horn sheep, mountain goats, and deer. Whether fishing, boating, mountain climbing, horseback riding, camping, biking, backpacking or hiking, this area has endless opportunities for outdoor recreation.

These 75 hikes lie within a 70-mile drive of Bozeman and are organized by groups in the drainages and mountain ranges that surround the city. A wide range of scenery and ecosystems accommodates all levels of hikes, from relaxing creekside strolls to all-day, high-elevation outings. The trails have been chosen for their scenery, variety, and ability to be hiked within the day.

Most of the hikes are accessed by three main routes—Highway 191 through the Gallatin Canyon, Highway 86 to the Bridgers, and Highway 89 through Paradise Valley. Within the city itself are 21 hikes.

To the north of Bozeman lies the Bridger Range, home to the Bridger Foothills National Recreation Trail and Bridger Bowl Ski Area. Many hiking and biking trails are found in this scenic mountain range because of its close proximity to Bozeman, yet this area retains a feeling of remoteness. Hikes 1—13 are located within the Bridgers.

Hikes 14—34 are in Bozeman or within a few minutes drive. The city lies in the East Gallatin Valley between the Bridgers and the Gallatin Range. Bozeman itself has a great variety of trails developed by the Gallatin Valley Land Trust. (See page 45 for more information.) Several trails access the nearby canyons and mountains from this community trail system.

South of Bozeman is the 34,000-acre Hyalite Drainage, a stunning mountain valley between the Gallatin Canyon and Paradise Valley. This drainage is a popular recreational area with a large reservoir built in the 1940s as its centerpiece. The Hyalite Reservoir has a holding capacity of 8,000 acre-feet of water and is used for drinking water for the city of Bozeman and to irrigate the Gallatin Valley. Its coves, creeks, and piers offer great trout fishing and boating opportunities. The Hyalite Drainage Recreational Area is surrounded by 10,000-foot mountain peaks and includes a large variety of biking and hiking trails, creeks, streams, lakes and numerous waterfalls. Hikes 35—46 lie in this beautiful mountain valley.

Hike 47 is located in Bear Trap Canyon in the Madison River drainage west of Bozeman. The canyon is a well known fishing and hiking area in a remote, roadless region within the Madison Range.

Hikes 48—58 are accessed from Highway 191 through the Gallatin Valley. Highway 191 snakes south through the Gallatin Canyon along the Gallatin River. The highway connects Bozeman with Big Sky and West Yellowstone, the west entrance to Yellowstone National Park. The Gallatin River and Highway 191 lie between two mountain ranges. To the east is the Gallatin Range, which includes the Hyalite Drainage. To the west is the Madison Range, which includes the Lee Metcalf Wilderness and the Spanish Peaks.

Several of the hikes are located in the rugged 78,000-acre Spanish Peaks Wilderness Area (part of the Lee Metcalf Wilderness), north of Big Sky and west of Highway 191. The steep Spanish Peaks contain some of the oldest rocks in North America. The three-billion year old metamorphic rocks were sculpted by glaciers, wind, and water. Within the area are 25 peaks rising above 10,000 feet, including Gallatin Peak at 11,015 feet. Below the peaks are wide subalpine meadows, forested valleys, and more than 175 lakes.

Continuing south on Highway 191 leads toward the headwaters of the Gallatin River and the far northwest corner of Yellowstone National Park. Hikes 59—67 are located along several tributaries of the Gallatin, traveling up through valleys to sweeping views of the landscape.

Highway 89 begins about 20 miles east of Bozeman at Livingston. The highway parallels the Yellowstone River through Paradise Valley, a wide, scenic valley flanked by majestic mountain peaks. Hikes 68—75 are accessed from Highway 89. The 53-mile stretch connects Livingston with Gardiner at the north entrance of Yellowstone Park. The valley is bordered by the Gallatin Range on the west and the Absaroka Range on the east.

A quick glance at the hikes' summaries will allow you to choose a hike that is appropriate to your ability and desire. An overall map on the next page identifies the locations of most of the hikes. Several other regional maps, as well as maps for each hike, provide the essential details. Many commercial maps are available for further hiking. Suggestions are listed with each hike and on page 8.

Even though these trails are described as day hikes, many of the trails involve serious backcountry hiking. Reference the hiking statistics listed at the top of each page for an approximation of difficulty, and match the hikes to your ability. Hiking times are calculated for continuous hiking. Allow extra time for exploration. Feel free to hike farther than these day hike suggestions, but be sure to carry additional trail and topographic maps. Use good judgement about your capabilities, and be prepared with adequate clothing and supplies.

Many of these hikes are located in high altitude terrain. Be aware that the increased elevation affects your stamina. Weather conditions undoubtedly change throughout the day and seasons. It is imperative to wear warm, layered clothing. Snacks, water, and a basic first aid kit are a must. Both black and grizzly bears inhabit the region, so wear a bear bell and hike in a group whenever possible. Some preparation and forethought will help ensure a safe, enjoyable, and memorable hike.

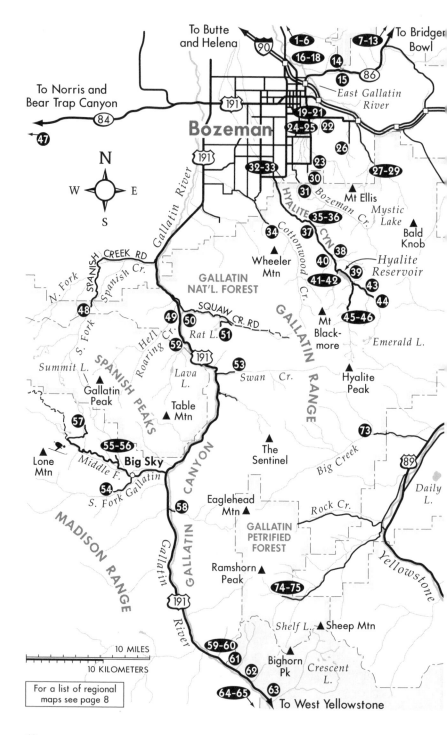

To Butte
and Helena

To Bridger
Bowl

1-6

7-13

16-18

14

15

86

To Norris and
Bear Trap Canyon

84

47

N

W   E

S

191

Bozeman

191

*East Gallatin
River*

19-21

24-25   22

26

27-29

32-33

23

30

31

35-36

Mt Ellis

*Mystic
Lake*

Bald
Knob

34

37

38

*Hyalite
Reservoir*

Wheeler
Mtn

40

39

43

41-42

44

Gallatin River

GALLATIN
NAT'L. FOREST

SPANISH CREEK RD

N. Fork

Spanish Cr.

SQUAW CR. RD

48

S. Fork

Hell

Roaring Cr.

49   50

Rat L.   51

Mt
Black-
more

45-46

Emerald L.

52

191

53

Swan   Cr.

Hyalite
Peak

Summit L.

SPANISH PEAKS

*Lava
L.*

Gallatin
Peak

57

*Table
Mtn*

73

55-56

Big Sky

Middle F.

GALLATIN CANYON

The
Sentinel

Big Creek

89

*Daily
L.*

Lone
Mtn

54

S. Fork Gallatin

58

Eaglehead
Mtn

Rock Cr.

GALLATIN
PETRIFIED
FOREST

Yellowstone

MADISON RANGE

GALLATIN RANGE

191

Gallatin

Ramshorn
Peak

74-75

River

Shelf L.   Sheep Mtn

59-60

61

Bighorn
Pk

*Crescent
L.*

62

63

64-65

To West Yellowstone

10 MILES

10 KILOMETERS

For a list of regional
maps see page 8

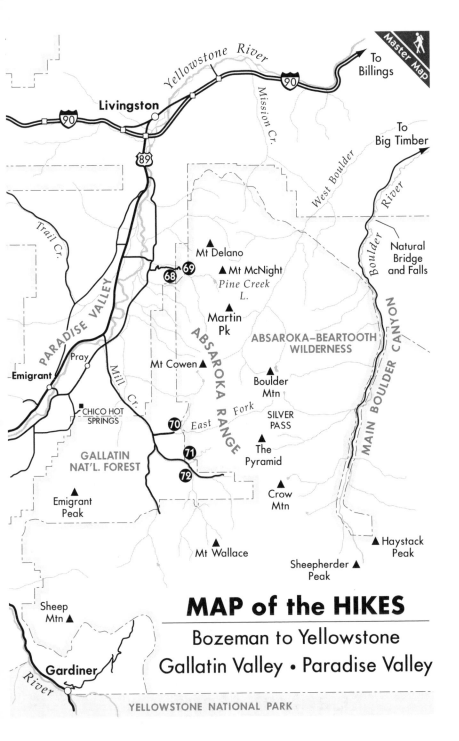

To Billings

Yellowstone River

Livingston

To Big Timber

Mission Cr.

West Boulder

Natural Bridge and Falls

Trail Cr.

Mt Delano

68 69

Mt McNight

Pine Creek L.

Martin Pk

ABSAROKA–BEARTOOTH WILDERNESS

Boulder

River

MAIN BOULDER CANYON

PARADISE VALLEY

Pray

Emigrant

Mill Cr.

Mt Cowen

ABSAROKA RANGE

East Fork

Boulder Mtn

SILVER PASS

CHICO HOT SPRINGS

70

71

72

The Pyramid

GALLATIN NAT'L. FOREST

Crow Mtn

Emigrant Peak

Mt Wallace

Sheepherder Peak

Haystack Peak

Sheep Mtn

Gardiner

River

MAP of the HIKES

Bozeman to Yellowstone
Gallatin Valley • Paradise Valley

YELLOWSTONE NATIONAL PARK

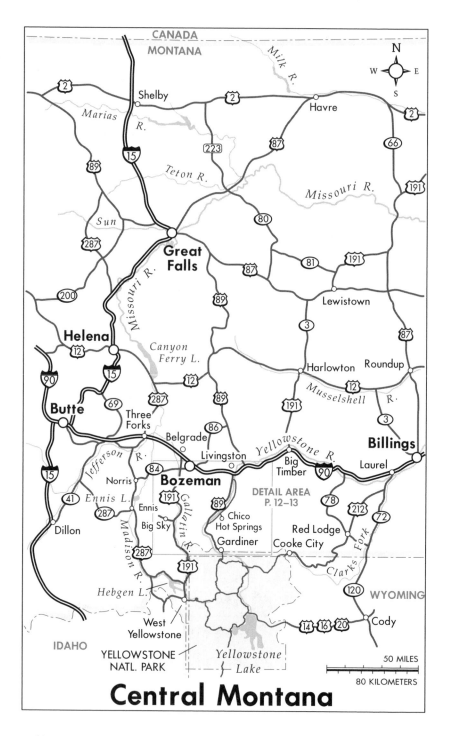

Central Montana

Bridger Mountains
and Bangtail Mountains

HIKES 1—13

map
next page

The Bridger Mountains abruptly rise from the north end of Bozeman, forming a backdrop for the city. The 25-mile-long range is a steep fold of sedimentary rock with a distinct rolling spine. The elevation ranges from 5,000 feet up to 9,665 feet at Sacagawea Peak, the highest peak in the range (Hike 10). The range borders the fertile Gallatin Valley on the west and the Bangtail Mountains to the east, divided by Bridger Canyon.

The Bridgers are surrounded by six mountain ranges. The Gallatin and Madison stretch to the south, the Crazies lie to the east, the Big Belts are to the north, the Elkhorns lie to the northwest, and the Tobacco Roots extend along the west. From atop the ridge, these mountain ranges can all be viewed.

The Bridger Foothills National Recreation Trail parallels the ridge in a steady series of ups and downs, skirting the west side of the peaks. The trail runs 24 miles, from Baldy Mountain, at the "M" picnic area on the south end of the Bridger Range (Hike 14), to Hardscrabble Peak (Hike 9).

The Bangtail Mountains to the east are a short range within the Bridger Mountains. The Bangtails lie between Bridger Canyon and Shields Valley, north of Bozeman Pass. The mountain range has a network of logging roads and hiking/biking trails.

Hikes 1—6 explore the west side of the Bridgers, accessed from the Gallatin Valley. Hikes 7—11 travel up the east side of the range from Bridger Canyon. Most of these hikes access the spine of the range and the Bridger Foothills National Recreation Trail, forming an interconnected network of trails. Hikes 12—13 begin in Bridger Canyon and head eastward into the Bangtail Mountains.

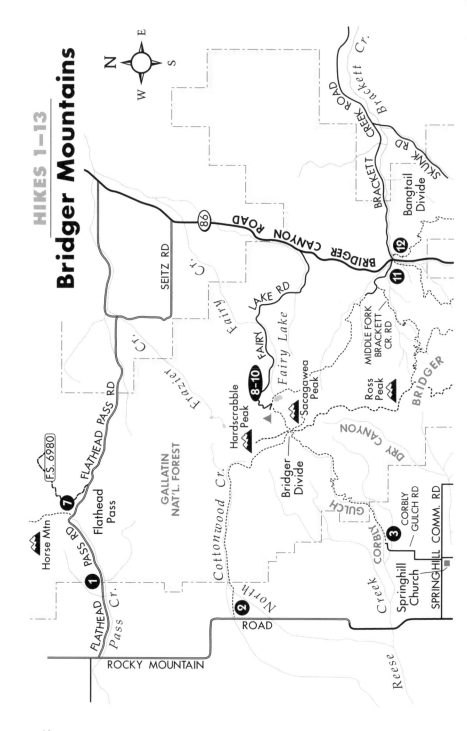

N
W E S

86

SEITZ RD

BRACKETT CREEK ROAD

SKUNK RD

Brackett Cr.

Bangtail Divide

12

BRIDGER CANYON ROAD

11

Fairy Cr.

FAIRY LAKE RD

Fairy Lake

MIDDLE FORK BRACKETT CR. RD

8-10

Sacagawea Peak

Ross Peak

BRIDGER

Hardscrabble Peak

F.S. 6980

FLATHEAD PASS RD

7

Horse Mtn

Flathead Pass

GALLATIN NAT'L. FOREST

Frazier Cr.

Cottonwood Cr.

Bridger Divide

DRY CANYON

GULCH

CORBLY

3

CORBLY GULCH RD

Springhill Church

SPRINGHILL COMM. RD

PASS RD

1

FLATHEAD Pass Cr.

North

2

ROAD

ROCKY MOUNTAIN

Reese Creek

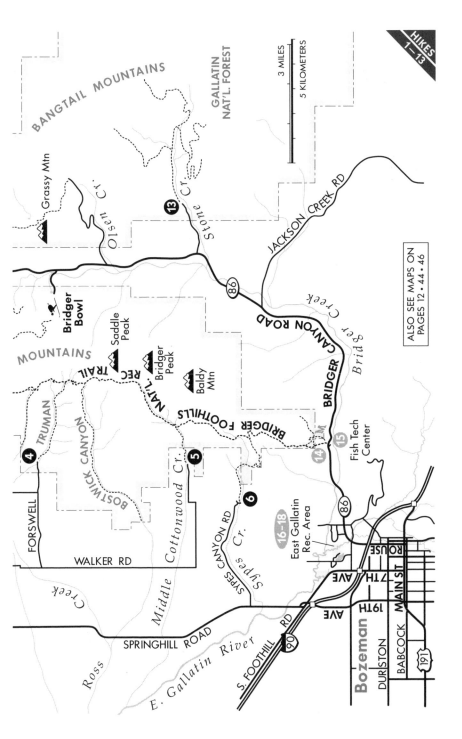

1. Flathead Pass

Hiking distance: 4.6 miles round trip
Hiking time: 2.5 hours
Elevation gain: 1,200 feet
Maps: U.S.G.S. Flathead Pass
        Beartooth Publishing: Bozeman, Big Sky, W. Yellowstone

Summary of hike: Flathead Pass crosses the north end of the Bridger Mountains, connecting the Gallatin Valley on the east with Bridger Canyon on the west. At the 6,922-foot pass is a top-of-the-world meadow covered in wildflowers, with stunning views of the surrounding peaks, Shields Valley, Gallatin Valley, and the Crazy Mountains. The trail is a forested road that hugs Pass Creek and steadily climbs past jagged rock walls and chiseled outcroppings. The narrow road can be driven, but is rutted and rocky. It is better explored as a hiking or biking route.

Driving directions: From I-90 and the 7th Avenue overpass, drive 2 miles north on 7th Avenue (which becomes West Frontage Road) to Springhill Road. Turn right (north) and continue 19.3 miles to posted Flathead Pass Road. (En route, the pavement ends at 11.3 miles and becomes Rocky Mountain Road.) Turn right and drive 2.1 miles on the narrow dirt road to the national forest boundary. Park on the side of the road.

Hiking directions: Head east on the narrow dirt road above Johnson Canyon to the south, and enter the shaded forest. Parallel the north side of Pass Creek, steadily gaining elevation and passing unmarked side roads that veer off from the main trail. At a half mile, pass Trail 528 on the left. Walk through sloping meadows with wildflowers and tree-shaded pockets. Cross under power poles at 0.8 miles by jagged rock walls and chiseled outcroppings in a gorge. Pass through a cattle gate and climb to the open, rolling meadows to Flathead Pass by a fenceline and cattle guard. The vistas extend across Shields Valley to the Crazy Mountains in the east and the Gallatin Valley and Tobacco Root

Mountains to the west. This is the turn-around spot.

To extend the hike, continue with Hike 7, heading north from the pass.

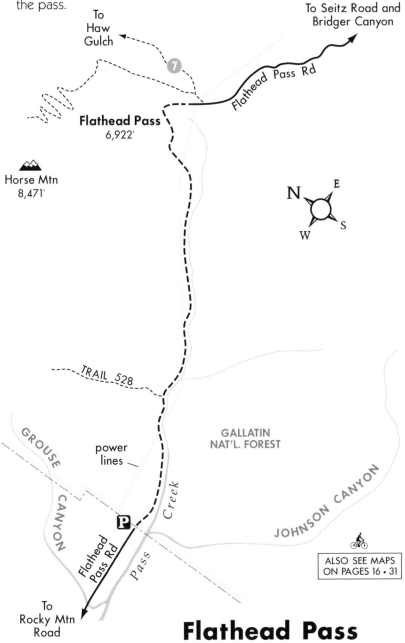

To Haw Gulch

To Seitz Road and Bridger Canyon

Flathead Pass Rd

Flathead Pass
6,922'

Horse Mtn
8,471'

N
E
W
S

TRAIL 528

GROUSE CANYON

power lines

GALLATIN NAT'L. FOREST

JOHNSON CANYON

Creek

Pass

Flathead Pass Rd

ALSO SEE MAPS ON PAGES 16 · 31

To Rocky Mtn Road

Flathead Pass

2. North Cottonwood Creek

Hiking distance: 8 miles round trip
Hiking time: 4 hours
Elevation gain: 2,000 feet

*map
next page*

Maps: U.S.G.S. Flathead Pass and Sacagawea Peak
Beartooth Publishing: Bozeman, Big Sky, W. Yellowstone

Summary of hike: North Cottonwood Creek forms at 8,700 feet on the north slope of Hardscrabble Peak. The cascading creek tumbles down the canyon en route to the Gallatin Valley. This hike follows the whitewater up the lush canyon, passing small waterfalls and pools to a huge meadow with wildflowers. The 7,700-foot tree-rimmed meadow sits beneath the shadow of Hardscrabble Peak. The trail crosses North Cottonwood Creek three times. The first mile traverses the grassy valley slope through Half Circle Ranch to the national forest boundary at the mouth of the canyon. The access is a ranch privilege, not an easement. Stay on the trail and help keep the access open. This trail can be hiked as an 8-mile, one-way shuttle to Fairy Lake (Hike 8).

Driving directions: From I-90 and the 7th Avenue overpass, drive 2 miles north on 7th Avenue (which becomes West Frontage Road) to Springhill Road. Turn right (north) and continue 14.5 miles to the posted trailhead parking area on the right. (En route, the pavement ends at 11.3 miles and becomes Rocky Mountain Road.)

Hiking directions: Walk through the trailhead gate, and cross the open grassland towards the mountains. The rock-embedded path parallels the ranch fenceline. At 0.7 miles, rock-hop or wade across North Cottonwood Creek. Merge with an old two-track wagon road. Pass through a gate and follow the creek into the mouth of the forested canyon and the gated U.S. forest boundary. Pass through the gate and follow the tumbling whitewater along a series of cascades, small waterfalls, and pools. At 2.3 miles, wade across the creek and follow the north side. Cross 2 tributary streams from the north canyon slope, and cross back to the south side of the creek at 3.5 miles. Climb high above the creek on the north-facing wall to a large forested flat with a trickling stream. Cross the stream a couple of times, and follow the stream's north edge through a sloping meadow beneath Hardscrabble Peak. Curve right around Peak 8558, and follow cairns through the trail-less meadow. This is the turn-around spot.

To extend the hike, the trail steadily climbs 2 more miles, gaining 1,000 feet to the Bridger Foothills National Recreation Trail at Bridger Divide, located in the saddle between Hardscrabble Peak and Sacagawea Peak.

3. Corbly Gulch

Hiking distance: 4 miles round trip
Hiking time: 2.5 hours
Elevation gain: 1,500 feet

map
next page

Maps: U.S.G.S. Miser Creek, Flathead Pass and Sacagawea Peak
Beartooth Publishing: Bozeman, Big Sky, W. Yellowstone

Summary of hike: Corbly Creek flows from the west slope of Sacagawea Peak, joining Limestone Creek and Reese Creek on its journey to the East Gallatin River. The trail up Corbly Gulch follows the creek past its headwaters to the Bridger Foothills National Recreation Trail on the saddle between Hardscrabble Peak and Sacagawea Peak. This hike follows the lower 2 miles of the trail from the mouth of the canyon in the Gallatin Valley. The trail leads through forests and meadows beneath the craggy canyon walls and crosses the creek many times to overlooks of the valley and Tobacco Root Mountains.

This trail can be hiked as an 8-mile, one-way shuttle to Fairy Lake (Hike 8).

Driving directions: From I-90 and the 7th Avenue overpass, drive 2 miles north on 7th Avenue (which becomes West Frontage Road) to Springhill Road. Turn right (north) and continue

8.5 miles to Springhill Community Road on the right. Turn right and drive 1.5 miles to Corbly Gulch Road, just before reaching the Springhill Church. Turn left on the gravel road and zigzag 2 miles to the posted trailhead access on the left. Turn left and park in the spaces on the right.

Hiking directions: Walk up the rutted two-track road through the open grasslands toward distinct Corbly Gulch. Parallel and cross Corbly Creek, steadily gaining elevation to the mouth of the canyon and the national forest boundary. Follow the north wall of the canyon and pass through a wire gate. Climb through flowered meadows with views of the Bridger Divide. Rock-hop or balance on logs across the creek, and weave uphill to vistas across the Gallatin Valley to the Tobacco Root Mountains. Enter the shade of a pine forest, passing small meadows. Curve left, following a trail sign to the creek. Cross the creek and follow the north edge of the cascading water. At 2 miles, the trail begins zigzagging across the creek six times. This is a good turn-around spot.

To extend the hike, the trail steadily climbs 4 more miles, gaining 2,500 feet to the Bridger Foothills National Recreation Trail at Bridger Divide, between Hardscrabble Peak and Sacagawea Peak.

HIKE 2
North Cottonwood Creek
HIKE 3
Corbly Gulch

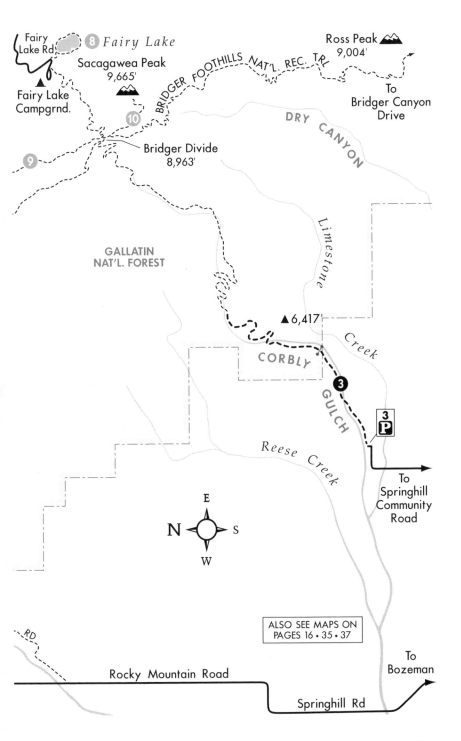

Fairy
Lake Rd

⑧ *Fairy Lake*

Ross Peak 🞁🞁
9,004'

Sacagawea Peak
9,665'

BRIDGER FOOTHILLS NAT'L. REC. TRL.

To
Bridger Canyon
Drive

▲
Fairy Lake
Campgrnd.

DRY CANYON

⑩

Bridger Divide
8,963'

⑨

Limestone

GALLATIN
NAT'L. FOREST

▲6,417'

Creek

CORBLY

❸

3
P

GULCH

Reese Creek

To
Springhill
Community
Road

E

N ✦ S

W

ALSO SEE MAPS ON
PAGES 16 • 35 • 37

To
Bozeman

RD

Rocky Mountain Road

Springhill Rd

4. Truman Gulch Trail

Hiking distance: 5 miles round trip
Hiking time: 2.5 hours
Elevation gain: 1,000 feet
Maps: U.S.G.S. Saddle Peak
U.S.F.S. Gallatin National Forest: West Half or East Half

Summary of hike: Truman Gulch sits on the west slope of the Bridger Mountains eight miles north of Bozeman. The stream-fed drainage is tucked between 9,004-foot Ross Peak and 9,159-foot Saddle Peak, directly west of Bridger Bowl Ski Area on the Gallatin Valley side of the range. The Truman Gulch Trail begins at the mouth of the canyon and climbs to the Bridger Foothills National Recreation Trail below the divide. The trail is surrounded by forested, rolling mountains and follows the course of the creek to overlooks with sweeping vistas. En route are three creek crossings.

Driving directions: From I-90 and the 7th Avenue overpass, drive 2 miles north on 7th Avenue (which becomes West Frontage Road) to Springhill Road. Turn right (north) and continue 8.5 miles to Springhill Community Road on the right. There is a sign for Truman Gulch. Turn right and continue 1.6 miles to Walker Road. The Springhill Church is on this corner. Turn right and drive 1.1 mile to Forswell Road and turn left. Continue 3 miles to the trailhead parking area at road's end.

Hiking directions: Head east into the canyon on the wide trail and pass a horse gate. Cross the creek at 0.2 miles and gradually climb through the forest. Cross the stream two more times at 1.8 miles. A short distance ahead, views open up of the surrounding mountains and several drainages converge. Cross the stream and climb steeply out of the valley for a half mile to the junction with the Bridger Foothills National Recreation Trail at 2.5 miles. This is the turn-around spot.

To hike farther, the right fork (south) connects with Bostwick

Canyon and Middle Cottonwood Creek Trail
(Hike 5). The left fork (north) leads to Ross
Pass (Hike 11).

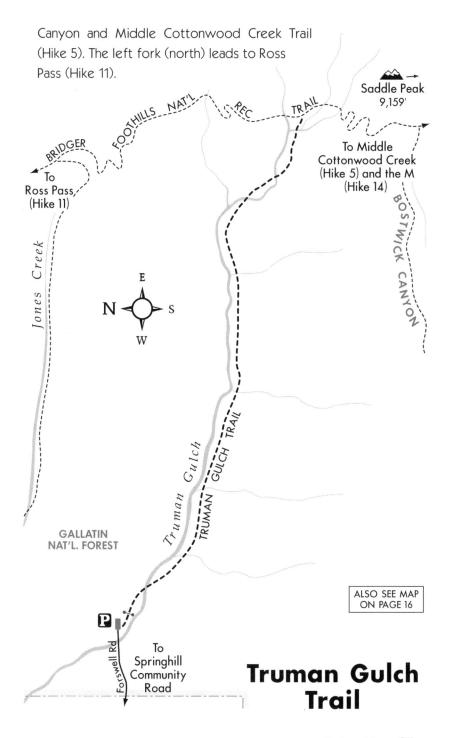

Saddle Peak
9,159'

To Middle
Cottonwood Creek
(Hike 5) and the M
(Hike 14)

To
Ross Pass
(Hike 11)

BOSTWICK CANYON

BRIDGER

FOOTHILLS NAT'L REC TRAIL

Jones Creek

Truman Gulch

TRUMAN GULCH TRAIL

GALLATIN
NAT'L. FOREST

ALSO SEE MAP
ON PAGE 16

Forswell Rd

To
Springhill
Community
Road

Truman Gulch
Trail

5. Middle Cottonwood Creek

Hiking distance: 2.8 miles round trip
Hiking time: 1.5 hours
Elevation gain: 450 feet
Maps: U.S.G.S. Miser Creek and Saddle Peak
U.S.F.S. Gallatin National Forest: West Half or East Half

Summary of hike: Middle Cottonwood Creek begins in the Bridger Mountains on the upper west slope of Saddle Peak. The creek cascades through the canyon to the Gallatin Valley and joins the East Gallatin River. This hike begins at the mouth of the canyon and follows the cascading whitewater of Middle Cottonwood Creek. The trail climbs toward Saddle Peak through lush riparian vegetation, passing colorful rock formations, small waterfalls, and pools. En route, the trail crosses the creek five times.

Driving directions: From I-90 and the 7th Avenue overpass, drive 2 miles north on 7th Avenue (which becomes West Frontage Road) to Springhill Road. Turn right (north) and continue 3.4 miles to Toohey Road on the right. There is a sign for Middle Cottonwood Creek. Turn right and drive 1.7 miles to Walker Road. Turn right again and continue 3.2 miles to the trailhead parking area at road's end.

Hiking directions: Head east past large boulders, and cross a footbridge over Middle Cottonwood Creek. Continue up the canyon, and cross a log over the creek at 0.4 miles. Follow the course of the creek past cascades and pools. The canyon narrows at 0.8 miles. Boulder hop to the north side of the creek amid moss-covered rock formations. At one mile, the trail joins the Bridger Foothills National Recreation Trail. To the right, the trail crosses the creek and heads 6 miles south to the M Trail (Hike 14). Continue straight ahead up the canyon. Zigzag up Baldy Mountain to a ridge overlooking the surrounding drainages at 1.4 miles. This is the turn-around spot.

To hike farther, the trail traverses the west slope of Bridger Peak and Saddle Peak on the Bridger Foothills National Recreation Trail, connecting with Bostwick Canyon and Truman Gulch (Hike 4).

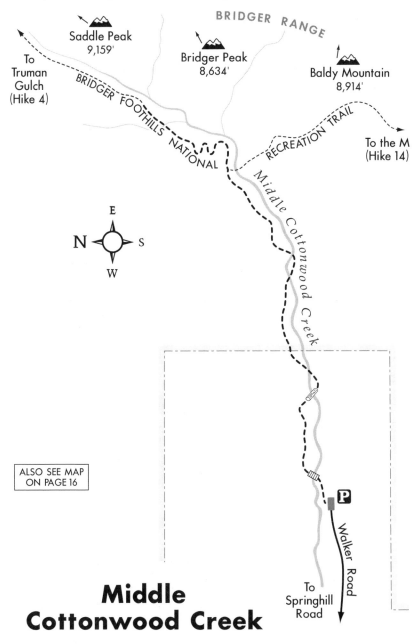

BRIDGER RANGE

Saddle Peak
9,159'

To
Truman
Gulch
(Hike 4)

BRIDGER FOOTHILLS NATIONAL

Bridger Peak
8,634'

Baldy Mountain
8,914'

RECREATION TRAIL

To the M
(Hike 14)

Middle Cottonwood Creek

N E S W

ALSO SEE MAP
ON PAGE 16

P

Walker Road

To
Springhill
Road

Middle
Cottonwood Creek

6. Sypes Canyon Trail

Hiking distance: 4 miles round trip
Hiking time: 2 hours
Elevation gain: 1,000 feet
Maps: U.S.G.S. Bozeman and Kelly Creek
U.S.F.S. Gallatin National Forest: West Half or East Half

Summary of hike: Sypes Canyon is located on the southwest flank of Baldy Mountain at the southern end of the Bridger Mountains. The Sypes Canyon Trail begins at the edge of the Gallatin Valley and climbs up the creek-fed canyon to the Bridger Foothills National Recreation Trail. The hike leads through a lush, shady forest up the south canyon wall to an overlook. From the overlook are great vistas of Bozeman; the expansive Gallatin Valley; and the Madison, Gallatin, and Tobacco Root mountain ranges.

Driving directions: From I-90 and the 7th Avenue overpass, drive 2 miles north on 7th Avenue (which becomes West Frontage Road) to Springhill Road. Turn right and drive 1.5 miles to Sypes Canyon Road. Turn right and continue 3.2 miles to Churn Road. Turn right and go 50 yards to the signed trailhead at the end of the road.

Hiking directions: Head east past the trail sign and through a grassy fenced access. Enter a lush forest canopy into Sypes Canyon on the right side of Sypes Creek. Cross over to the north side of the creek, and head up the north wall of the canyon above Sypes Creek. At a half mile, the trail reaches a ridge. Descend alongside a rock wall cliff into the lush, forested canyon. Curve right at one mile, heading south up the canyon while skirting the edge of the national forest boundary. Begin an ascent through a lodgepole pine forest to a saddle by a trail sign with a view of the valley. Bear left 200 yards to an overlook of Bozeman and the Madison Range. This is a great spot to relax and enjoy the views before returning back down Sypes Canyon.

To hike farther, the trail climbs one mile to a cairn-marked junction with the Bridger Foothills National Recreation Trail. The right fork descends to the M Trail at the south end of the Bridger Mountains (Hike 14). The left fork climbs to the head of Middle Cottonwood Creek (Hike 5).

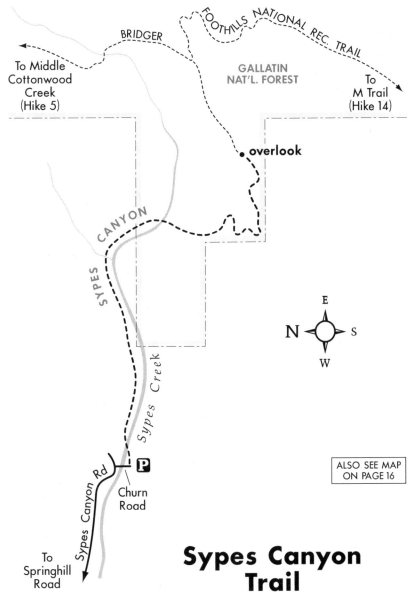

BRIDGER

FOOTHILLS NATIONAL REC. TRAIL

To Middle
Cottonwood
Creek
(Hike 5)

GALLATIN
NAT'L. FOREST

To
M Trail
(Hike 14)

• **overlook**

CANYON

SYPES

Sypes Creek

E
N ← ⬦ → S
W

Sypes Canyon Rd

P

Churn
Road

ALSO SEE MAP
ON PAGE 16

To
Springhill
Road

Sypes Canyon Rd

Sypes Canyon Trail

7. Horse Mountain Traverse

Hiking distance: 2.8 miles round trip
Hiking time: 1.5 hours
Elevation gain: 100 feet
Maps: U.S.G.S. Flathead Pass and Blacktail Mountain
Beartooth Publishing: Bozeman, Big Sky, W. Yellowstone

Summary of hike: The Horse Mountain Traverse is an easy hike through meadows atop Flathead Pass at 6,922 feet. The near-level path traverses the east flank of Horse Mountain on an old logging road reclaimed by vegetation. The trail leads to an open grassy saddle at the headwaters of Haw Gulch. From the saddle are vistas of Horsethief Mountain, Shields Valley, and the Crazy Mountains.

Driving directions: From Main Street in downtown Bozeman, head north on North Rouse Avenue. Drive 25.2 miles up Bridger Canyon to Seitz Road on the left. It is located 3.8 miles past Fairy Lake Road. (En route, the road becomes Bridger Canyon Drive/Highway 86.) Drive 4.3 miles on the unpaved road to a signed junction. Turn left towards Flathead Pass, and continue 5.9 miles to the pass. Along the way, stay left at a fork with F.S. Road 6980. At the pass, cross a cattle guard to the power poles. Park on the right.

Hiking directions: From the gorgeous meadow, veer north on the dirt road under the power poles. Head up the flower-covered meadow 100 yards to a Y-fork. The left fork leads to a knoll and steeply climbs Horse Mountain. Veer right and traverse the east slope of Horse Mountain. The old road meanders through meadows dotted with firs and pines at a near-level grade. At just over one mile, pass through a gated fence to a 7,000-foot saddle with north views of Horsethief Mountain. Easily descend, passing the Haw Gulch stream flowing under the trail. The trail abruptly ends in a dense pocket of pine trees at 1.4 miles.

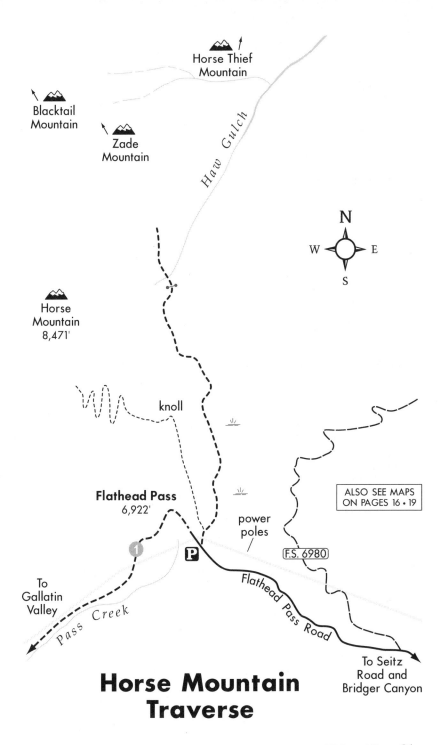

Horse Thief
Mountain

Blacktail
Mountain

Zade
Mountain

Haw Gulch

N
W E
S

Horse
Mountain
8,471'

knoll

Flathead Pass
6,922'

power
poles

ALSO SEE MAPS
ON PAGES 16 • 19

P

F.S. 6980

To
Gallatin
Valley

Pass Creek

Flathead Pass Road

To Seitz
Road and
Bridger Canyon

Horse Mountain
Traverse

8. Fairy Lake Trail

Hiking distance: 1.2 mile loop
Hiking time: 40 minutes
Elevation gain: 100 feet
Maps: U.S.G.S. Sacagawea Peak
U.S.F.S. Gallatin National Forest: East Half

Summary of hike: Fairy Lake is a picture-perfect, tree-lined lake sitting in a forested bowl at the base of Sacagawea Peak. The 20-acre lake receives heavy use due to its close proximity to the Fairy Lake Campground, located a short quarter mile away. The trail loops around the perimeter of the high mountain lake. It is a great place to have a picnic, fish for cutthroat trout, and spend the day.

Driving directions: From Main Street in downtown Bozeman, head north on North Rouse Avenue. Drive 21.4 miles up Bridger Canyon to the signed Fairy Lake turnoff on the left, 0.9 miles past the Battle Ridge Campground. (En route, the road becomes Bridger Canyon Drive/Highway 86). Turn left on Fairy Lake Road/Forest Service Road 74. Drive 6.1 miles on the unpaved road to the Fairy Lake Campground. Park at the signed trailhead on the left.

Hiking directions: Take the signed Fairy Lake Trail gently downhill for a quarter mile to the north shore of the lake. At the shoreline bear left, following the forested route along the east shore of the lake. Rock hop across Fairy Creek, the lake's outlet stream. A fisherman trail follows the shoreline, hugging the edge of the water. Various side paths meander through the forest and reconnect at the shoreline. Loop around to the west end of the lake. The path continues along the water's edge below the rocky sedimentary cliffs of Sacagawea Peak. After completing the loop, return to the left.

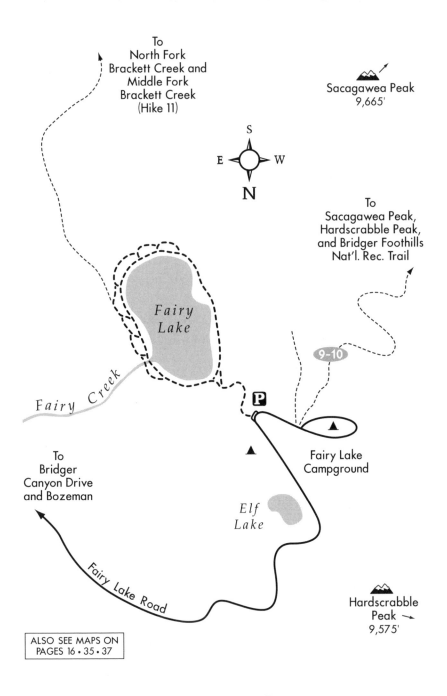

To
North Fork
Brackett Creek and
Middle Fork
Brackett Creek
(Hike 11)

Sacagawea Peak
9,665'

S

E W

N

To
Sacagawea Peak,
Hardscrabble Peak,
and Bridger Foothills
Nat'l. Rec. Trail

*Fairy
Lake*

9-10

Fairy Creek

P

To
Bridger
Canyon Drive
and Bozeman

▲

Fairy Lake
Campground

*Elf
Lake*

Fairy Lake Road

Hardscrabble
Peak →
9,575'

ALSO SEE MAPS ON
PAGES 16 • 35 • 37

Fairy Lake

9. Hardscrabble Peak

Hiking distance: 4 miles round trip
Hiking time: 3 hours
Elevation gain: 1,900 feet
Maps: U.S.G.S. Sacagawea Peak
U.S.F.S. Gallatin National Forest: East Half

Summary of hike: Hardscrabble Peak stands directly north of Sacagawea Peak in the northern Bridger Mountains. Frazier Lake and Ainger Lake sit on the east slope of the triple-peak mountain, 1,400 feet below. This hike leads to the summit of Hardscrabble Peak at 9,575 feet, gaining 1,900 feet en route. The trail follows the drainage between Sacagawea Peak and Hardscrabble Peak to the 8,963-foot saddle at Bridger Divide. From Hardscrabble Peak are views of six surrounding mountain ranges—the Gallatin, Madison, Crazies, Tobacco Roots, Elkhorns, and Big Belts.

Driving directions: From Main Street in downtown Bozeman, head north on North Rouse Avenue. Drive 21.4 miles up Bridger Canyon to the signed Fairy Lake turnoff on the left, 0.9 miles past the Battle Ridge Campground. (En route, the road becomes Bridger Canyon Drive/Highway 86). Turn left on Fairy Lake Road/Forest Service Road 74. Drive 6.1 miles on the unpaved road to the Fairy Lake Campground. Turn right and park 0.1 mile ahead at the signed trail on the left.

Hiking directions: Head south on the signed right fork through the shady forest. A series of switchbacks lead up the mountain, offering views to the east. Cross a grassy, wildflower-covered meadow, and begin the exposed climb up the rocky glacial cirque. Switchbacks lead up to the 8,963-foot ridge at the Bridger Divide, where there are cairns and a signed junction. The left fork (Hike 10) leads to Sacagawea Peak, the highest peak in the Bridger Mountains. Take the right fork and follow the ridge north, gaining another 675 feet from the saddle to the peak.

After marveling at the vistas from the rocky peak, return along the same path.

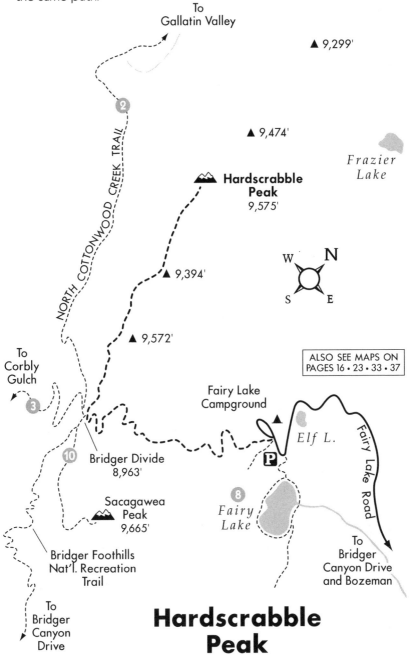

To Gallatin Valley

▲ 9,299'

▲ 9,474'

Frazier Lake

NORTH COTTONWOOD CREEK TRAIL

2

▲▲ **Hardscrabble Peak**
9,575'

W N
S E

▲ 9,394'

▲ 9,572'

To Corbly Gulch

3

ALSO SEE MAPS ON
PAGES 16 • 23 • 33 • 37

Fairy Lake Campground

▲

Elf L.

Fairy Lake Road

10 Bridger Divide
8,963'

P

Sacagawea
▲▲ Peak
9,665'

8

Fairy Lake

Bridger Foothills
Nat'l. Recreation
Trail

To Bridger
Canyon Drive
and Bozeman

To
Bridger
Canyon
Drive

Hardscrabble Peak

10. Sacagawea Peak

Hiking distance: 4 miles round trip
Hiking time: 3 hours
Elevation gain: 2,000 feet
Maps: U.S.G.S. Sacagawea Peak
U.S.F.S. Gallatin National Forest: East Half

Summary of hike: Sacagawea Peak, named after Lewis and Clark's Indian guide, is the highest peak in the Bridger Range. The 9,665-foot peak sits on the northern end of the range and can be accessed from the west on the North Cottonwood Creek Trail and the Corbly Gulch Trail (Hikes 2 and 3). The shortest and most popular route is this trail from the east, starting at the Fairy Lake Campground. The trail climbs the mountain, passing through a glacial cirque to Bridger Divide between Sacagawea Peak and Hardscrabble Peak. From the divide the trail winds up to the rocky summit for fantastic views of mountain ranges in every direction. To the south are the Gallatin and Madison Ranges; the Big Belts lie to the north; the Elkhorns and Tobacco Roots lie to the west; and the Crazies are to the east.

Driving directions: Same as Hike 9.

Hiking directions: From the signed trail, take the right fork through the conifer forest. Traverse the hillside up several switchbacks while great views open up to the east. Cross the northern edge of a meadow abundant with wildflowers. Switchbacks lead up the exposed rocky bowl at the head of the drainage. More switchbacks climb up to the ridge on the Bridger Divide at 8,963 feet. At the divide are cairns and a signed junction. The right fork leads up to Hardscrabble Peak (Hike 9). Take the left fork and follow the ridge south. Pass a signed junction on the right, heading down the mountain to Corbly Creek and North Cottonwood Creek. Continue gaining elevation southeast along the ridge. Bear left at a junction with the Bridger Foothills National Recreation Trail, and head north for the final ascent to the peak.

After enjoying the incredible views at the summit, return along the same path.

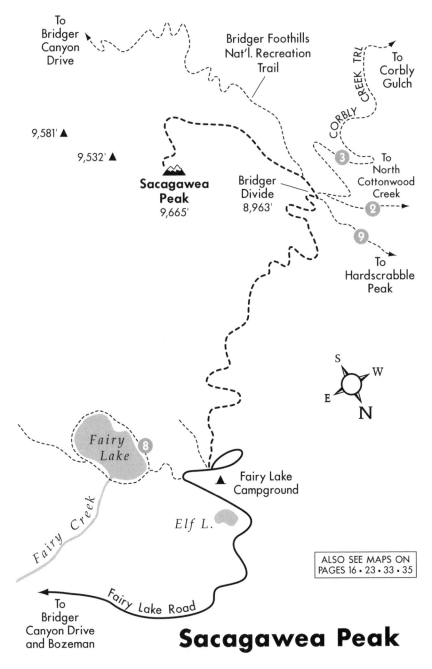

To
Bridger
Canyon
Drive

Bridger Foothills
Nat'l. Recreation
Trail

CORBLY CREEK TRL

To
Corbly
Gulch

9,581' ▲

9,532' ▲

Sacagawea
Peak
9,665'

Bridger
Divide
8,963'

3

To
North
Cottonwood
Creek

2

9

To
Hardscrabble
Peak

S W
E N

Fairy
Lake 8

Fairy Lake
Campground

Fairy Creek

Elf L.

ALSO SEE MAPS ON
PAGES 16 • 23 • 33 • 35

To
Bridger
Canyon Drive
and Bozeman

Fairy Lake Road

Sacagawea Peak

11. Middle Fork Brackett Creek to Ross Pass

Hiking distance: 6 to 12.5 miles round trip
Hiking time: 3 to 6 hours
Elevation gain: 1,400 to 1,800 feet
Maps: U.S.G.S. Saddle Peak
      Beartooth Publishing: Bozeman, Big Sky, W. Yellowstone

map
next page

Summary of hike: Ross Peak is a jagged 9,004-foot peak between Sacagawea Peak and Bridger Bowl Ski Area. Grass-covered Ross Pass sits on the south flank of Ross Peak in a long, sweeping arch. Atop the 7,620-foot alpine pass is the Bridger Foothills National Recreation Trail. Dramatic limestone formations lie just west of the ridge. The vistas are breathtaking. This hike begins in Bridger Canyon but can be shortened by driving up Middle Fork Brackett Creek Road. The road/trail roughly follows the creek, crossing feeder streams and passing its headwaters en route to Ross Pass.

Driving directions: From Main Street in downtown Bozeman, head north on North Rouse Avenue. Drive 18.8 miles up Bridger Canyon to posted Brackett Creek Road. It is located 2 miles past the Bridger Bowl Ski Area entrance between mile markers 18 and 19. (En route, the road becomes Bridger Canyon Drive/Highway 86.) Curve right on Brackett Creek Road 100 yards to the large Bangtail Divide Trailhead parking lot on the right.

This hike—Middle Fork Brackett Creek Road—is a primitive dirt road on the west side of Bridger Canyon. It can be comfortably driven for almost 3 miles. Thereafter, the old logging road gets steeper, narrower, and rutted and is not recommended for driving. These hiking directions start from the bottom, but can be shortened as you choose.

Hiking directions: Walk 100 yards down Brackett Creek Road to Highway 86. Pick up the posted Middle Fork Brackett Creek Road and head west, passing a narrow side road on the left. Skirt the east edge of an expansive sloping meadow with views of Ross Peak and Ross Pass. Loop around the north end of the meadow to a Y-fork at one mile. The right fork leads to Fairy Lake (Hike 8). Stay left to a metal gate at 1.8 miles, and follow the north edge of Middle Fork Brackett Creek. At 2.5 miles, wind steeply uphill to an overlook of Grassy Mountain in the Bangtail Mountains (Hike 12). Zigzag up the mountain, with continuous vistas of Ross Pass and Ross Peak. Cross a feeder stream and weave up to views of the Crazy Mountains. On a right bend, Trail 525 veers left, leading to South Fork Brackett Creek and Bridger Bowl. Climb 4 long switchbacks toward the pass. Traverse the slope to a large flower-filled meadow below the saddle. Make the final steep ascent to posted Ross Pass and a T-junction with the Bridger Foothills National Recreation Trail at 7,640 feet. Just west of the pass are the gorgeous limestone fins. To the right (north), the trail leads to Sacagawea Peak. To the south, it leads towards Bridger Bowl.

12. Bangtail Divide Trail
GRASSY MOUNTAIN TRAIL

Hiking distance: 7.5 miles round trip
Hiking time: 4 hours
Elevation gain: 1,400 feet
Maps: U.S.G.S. Saddle Peak and Grassy Mountain
       Beartooth Publishing: Bozeman, Big Sky, W. Yellowstone

map next page

Summary of hike: The Bangtail Divide Trail (also called Grassy Mountain Trail) straddles the ridge dividing Bridger Canyon and Shields Valley. The 23-mile trail connects Brackett Creek in the north with Olson Creek and Stone Creek to the south (Hike 13). This hike follows the northern 3.5 miles of the trail, traversing Grassy Mountain through lodgepole pines and flower-filled meadows. The trail skirts the ridgeline and has sweeping vistas.

Driving directions: Follow the directions for Hike 11 to the Bangtail Divide Trailhead parking lot.

Hiking directions: Cross the footbridge over Brackett Creek, and curve left on the northern base of Grassy Mountain. Ten switchbacks zigzag up the slope, gaining a quick 400 feet. On the eighth switchback is an overlook of Ross Pass, Ross Peak, Sacagawea Peak, Hardscrabble Peak, and Horse Mountain. Head south, traversing the drainage on the cliffside path. Weave through the lodgepole pines, with frequent views of the Bridger Range and its jagged, sculpted

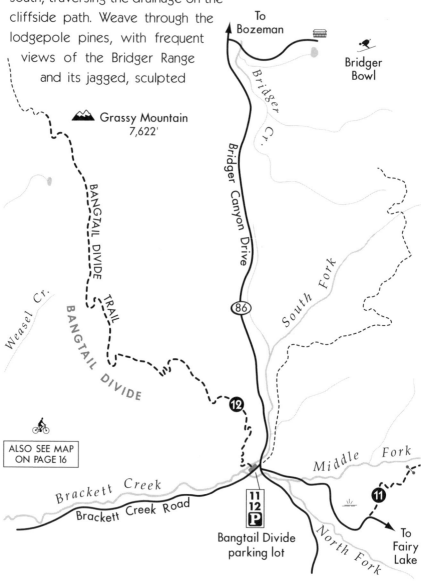

To Bozeman

Bridger Bowl

Grassy Mountain
7,622'

Bridger Cr.

Bridger Canyon Drive

BANGTAIL DIVIDE TRAIL

BANGTAIL DIVIDE

Weasel Cr.

86

South Fork

ALSO SEE MAP
ON PAGE 16

12

Brackett Creek

Brackett Creek Road

11
12
P

Bangtail Divide
parking lot

Middle Fork

11

North Fork

To Fairy Lake

peaks. Four more switchbacks lead to Bangtail Divide, with eastward views down Weasel Creek Canyon to Shields Valley and the Crazy Mountains. The trail levels out and weaves through meadows dotted with pines. The views include Battle Ridge in the north and Grassy Mountain to the south. Climb through the forest, returning to the divide. Follow the ridge south, and cross a saddle through a sloping meadow with a view across Bridger Canyon to Bridger Bowl and the ski runs. Descend on the east side of Grassy Mountain below the summit in a meadow at 3.7 miles, overlooking the logged area and network of roads far below. This is the turn-around spot. No routes lead up to the 7,622-foot peak.

To extend the hike, the trail descends to Skunk Creek Road at 7 miles and continues down to Olson Creek.

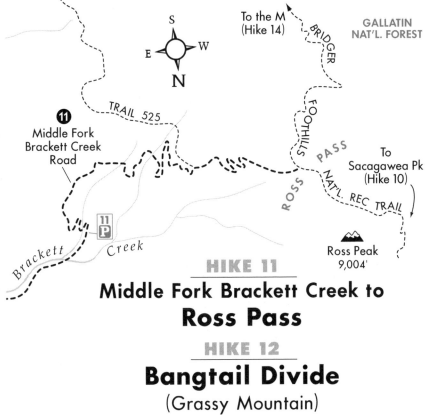

HIKE 11

Middle Fork Brackett Creek to
Ross Pass

HIKE 12
Bangtail Divide
(Grassy Mountain)

13. Stone Creek Trail

Hiking distance: 4 miles round trip
Hiking time: 2 hours
Elevation gain: 400 feet
Maps: U.S.G.S. Saddle Peak and Grassy Mountain
U.S.F.S. Gallatin National Forest: East Half or West Half

Summary of hike: Stone Creek Canyon is in the Bangtail Mountains on the east side of Bridger Canyon, directly south of Grassy Mountain. The creek begins at a 7,700-foot ridge and tumbles 2,300 feet downhill in 4.4 miles to Bridger Creek. The Stone Creek Trail winds through a beautiful rolling mountain and meadow landscape. It is more of a stroll through the mountains than a backcountry hike, as the trail begins on a vehicle-restricted logging road. The road heads up the drainage on a gradual incline along the north bank of cascading Stone Creek. This is also a popular cross-country ski trail.

Driving directions: From Main Street in downtown Bozeman, head north on North Rouse Avenue. Drive 12 miles up Bridger Canyon to Stone Creek Road on the right. (En route, the road becomes Bridger Canyon Drive/Highway 86.) Turn right and continue 1.2 miles to the Forest Service gate. Parking pullouts are located on both sides of the road.

Hiking directions: From the parking area, hike east up the forested canyon road past the Forest Service gate. At 0.5 miles, an old abandoned log house sits to the right of the trail by Stone Creek. At 1.2 miles, the Moody Creek Trail heads north up Moody Gulch. Stay on the Stone Creek Road to the end of the draw at 2 miles. The road curves sharply to the right and crosses Stone Creek, continuing to the right. A posted foot trail leaves the road at this curve and crosses the creek to the left. From here, the trail ascends steeply out of the canyon. This is the turn-around spot.

To continue, the trail gains 1,400 feet to the Bangtail Divide, overlooking the Bangtail Creek drainage, Shields Valley, and the Crazy Mountains.

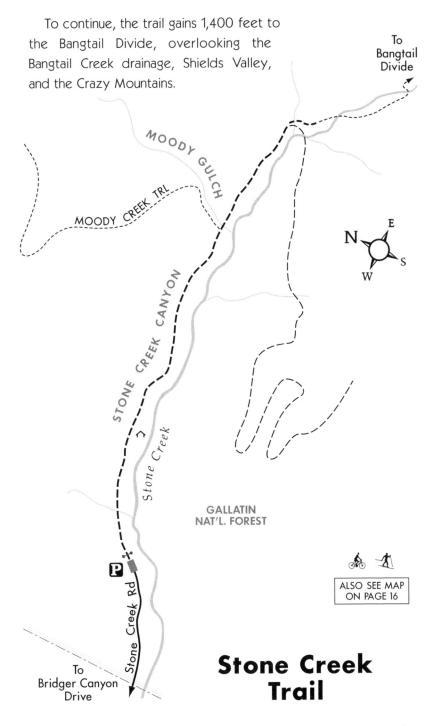

To Bangtail Divide

MOODY GULCH

MOODY CREEK TRL

STONE CREEK CANYON

Stone Creek

N E S W

GALLATIN NAT'L. FOREST

ALSO SEE MAP ON PAGE 16

P

Stone Creek Rd

To Bridger Canyon Drive

Stone Creek Trail

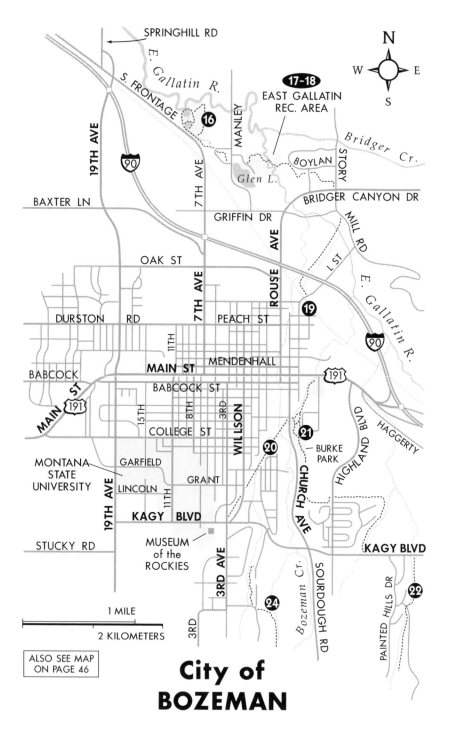

SPRINGHILL RD

E. Gallatin R.

S. FRONTAGE

N
W · E
S

17-18
EAST GALLATIN
REC. AREA

16

MANLEY

Bridger Cr.

BOYLAN

Glen L.

STORY

19TH AVE

90

7TH AVE

BRIDGER CANYON DR

BAXTER LN

GRIFFIN DR

ROUSE AVE

L ST

MILL RD

E. Gallatin R.

OAK ST

7TH AVE

90

19

DURSTON   RD

11TH

PEACH ST

BABCOCK

MAIN ST

MENDENHALL

191

MAIN ST

191

BABCOCK ST

15TH

8TH

3RD

WILLSON

COLLEGE ST

20

21
BURKE
PARK

MONTANA
STATE
UNIVERSITY

GARFIELD

19TH AVE

LINCOLN

11TH

GRANT

CHURCH AVE

HIGHLAND BLVD

HAGGERTY

KAGY   BLVD

STUCKY RD

MUSEUM
of the
ROCKIES

3RD AVE

KAGY BLVD

Bozeman Cr.

SOURDOUGH RD

PAINTED HILLS DR

22

1 MILE

24

2 KILOMETERS

3RD

ALSO SEE MAP
ON PAGE 46

City of
BOZEMAN

In and Around Bozeman

HIKES 14—34

map
next page

These 21 hikes lie within a 10-mile radius of Bozeman. They include several miles of hiking and biking routes within the open space of the city, which sits between mountain ranges in the East Gallatin Valley. The northern end of the Gallatin Range slopes down to the southeast end of Bozeman, offering many beautiful canyon hikes only a few minutes drive from downtown. The southern reaches of the Bridger Range curves toward Bozeman from the northeast. Hikes 14 and 15 are located at the end of this range at the large Montana State University "M."

The hikes within Bozeman itself are part of the Main Street to the Mountains trail system, developed and expanded by the hard work and dedication of the Gallatin Valley Land Trust (see below). Hikes 16—25 are part of this trail system, which accesses the East Gallatin Recreation Area, Burke Park, Highland Ridge, and Bozeman Creek.

Mount Ellis and Chestnut Mountain rise at Bozeman's southeast end. New World Gulch and Bear Creek drainages flow between the mountains, feeding the East Gallatin. Hikes 26—29 explore this fairly remote yet nearby area.

Bozeman Creek Road—Hike 30—is a popular destination for hiking, biking, and horse packing. To the west of this canyon is Leverich Canyon (Hike 31), Kirk Hill (Hikes 32—33), Hyalite Canyon (Hikes 35—47), and South Cottonwood Canyon (Hike 34).

The Gallatin Valley Land Trust (GVLT) is a non-profit organization dedicated to the protection and preservation of open space, including conservation easements, wildlife habitat, and the creation of public trails in and around Gallatin County. They are primarily responsible for building *Main Street to the Mountains*, Bozeman's community trail system. The trail network weaves through Bozeman's neighborhoods, connecting historic corridors, open grasslands, riparian waterways, and scenic ridgelines with views of the Gallatin Valley and surrounding peaks. The trails will eventually link downtown Bozeman with the Bridger Mountains and the Gallatins. Their efforts and accomplishments are largely due to volunteer labor, donations, and grants. To contact GVLT, call (406) 587-8404.

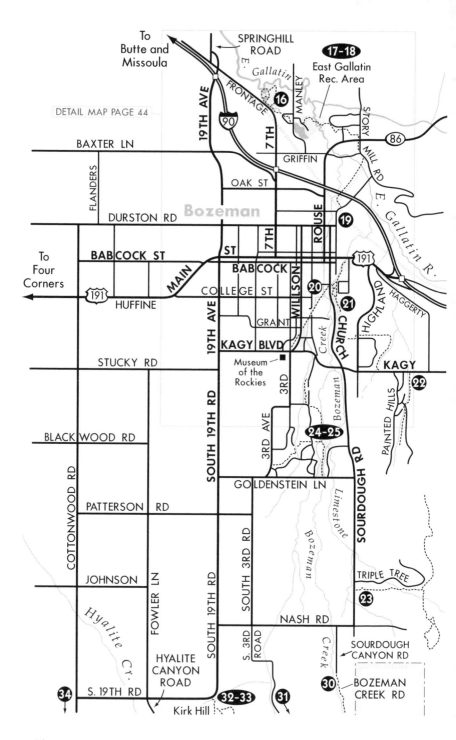

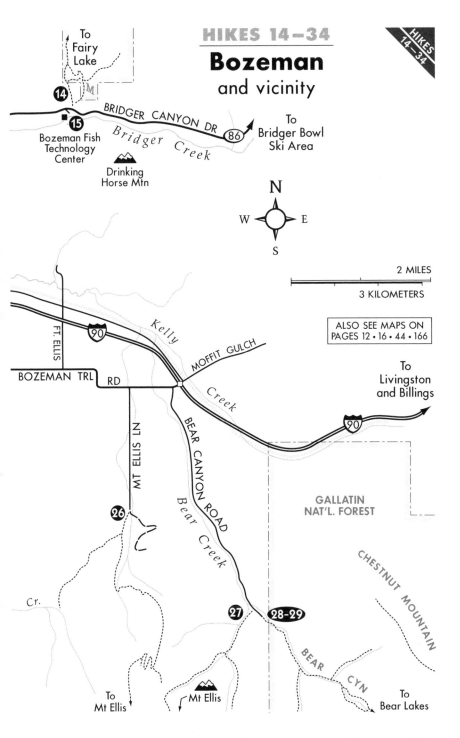

Bozeman
and vicinity

To
Fairy
Lake

14

BRIDGER CANYON DR

15 86

Bozeman Fish
Technology
Center

Bridger Creek

Drinking
Horse Mtn

To
Bridger Bowl
Ski Area

N
W E
S

2 MILES

3 KILOMETERS

ALSO SEE MAPS ON
PAGES 12 • 16 • 44 • 166

FT. ELLIS

90

Kelly

MOFFIT GULCH

BOZEMAN TRL   RD

Creek

To
Livingston
and Billings

90

MT ELLIS LN

BEAR CANYON ROAD

Bear Creek

GALLATIN
NAT'L. FOREST

26

Cr.

27

28-29

CHESTNUT MOUNTAIN

BEAR

CYN

To
Mt Ellis

Mt Ellis

To
Bear Lakes

14. M Trail

Hiking distance: 1.6 mile loop
Hiking time: 1 hour
Elevation gain: 850 feet
Maps: U.S.G.S. Kelly Creek
U.S.F.S. Gallatin National Forest: East Half

Summary of hike: The landmark Montana State University M is located at the mouth of Bridger Canyon on the south flanks of Baldy Mountain. The M was created by MSU students in 1915. The 250-foot whitewashed rock letter has two access routes. The right fork follows the ridge for a steep but direct route. The left fork switchbacks through a fir and juniper forest, making a more gradual ascent. The left fork is the beginning of the Bridger Foothills National Recreation Trail, a 24-mile ridge route following the contours of the Bridger Range. This hike to the M climbs up the steeper ridge route and descends through the forest via the switchbacks.

Driving directions: From Main Street in downtown Bozeman, head north on North Rouse Avenue 4.2 miles to the signed trailhead on the left, across from the fish hatchery. En route, the road curves right and becomes Bridger Canyon Drive (Highway 86). Turn left into the trailhead parking lot.

Hiking directions: Head north past the trailhead gate and picnic area to a junction with wide, clearly defined trails. Begin the loop by taking the right fork in a counter-clockwise direction. Head steeply up the ridge, hiking mercilessly up to the base of the M. Beyond the M is a junction. The right fork loops back to the top of the M and the ridge. The left fork levels out and begins the return loop. Bear left at a second junction and begin the descent on the switchbacks to a junction with the Bridger Foothills National Recreation Trail (Trail #534). Go left (south), returning to the base of the mountain and completing the loop. Return to the trailhead on the right.

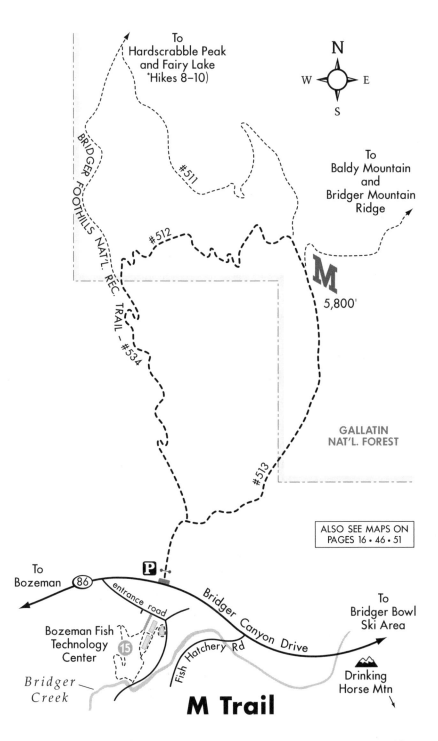

To
Hardscrabble Peak
and Fairy Lake
(Hikes 8–10)

N

W   E

S

BRIDGER FOOTHILLS NAT'L. REC. TRAIL – #534

#511

#512

To
Baldy Mountain
and
Bridger Mountain
Ridge

M
5,800'

GALLATIN
NAT'L. FOREST

#513

ALSO SEE MAPS ON
PAGES 16 • 46 • 51

P

To
Bozeman

86

entrance road

Bridger Canyon Drive

To
Bridger Bowl
Ski Area

Bozeman Fish
Technology
Center

15

Fish Hatchery Rd

Bridger
Creek

Drinking
Horse Mtn

M Trail

15. Bozeman Fish Technology Center Nature Trail

Open 8:00 a.m.—4:00 p.m. daily

Hiking distance: 0.5 mile loop
Hiking time: 30 minutes
Elevation gain: 50 feet
Maps: U.S.G.S. Kelly Creek
       Bozeman Fish Technology Center tour map

Summary of hike: The Bozeman Fish Technology Center sits at the base of Drinking Horse Mountain at the south end of the Bridger Mountains, across from the M Trail. The center is a hatchery and research area, including fish runs with observation walkways, a pond, and a picnic area. The hatchery borders Bridger Creek, a major tributary of the East Gallatin River. This hike follows a charming half-mile nature loop along Bridger Creek on the lower slopes of Drinking Horse Mountain.

Driving directions: From Main Street in downtown Bozeman, head north on North Rouse Avenue 4.1 miles to the signed Bozeman Fish Technology Center on the right, across the road from the M Trail (Hike 14). En route, the road curves right and becomes Bridger Canyon Drive/Highway 86. Turn right and park in the visitor parking lot on the right.

Hiking directions: Take the log-lined path west past the metal sculptures of cutthroat trout and graylings. Head up the hillside through the grove of aspens and wild roses to an overlook of the Montana State University M at a trail split (Hike 14). The right fork leads 20 yards and ends on a knoll. Bear left along the rolling hills, and descend to a wooden footbridge crossing a streambed. Go to the left and parallel Bridger Creek, heading upstream to the hatchery maintenance road. An arched bridge crosses the creek to the right to the housing area. Go to the left, following the road back to the parking lot. To the east of the parking lot are the fish raceways, the pond, and picnic area.

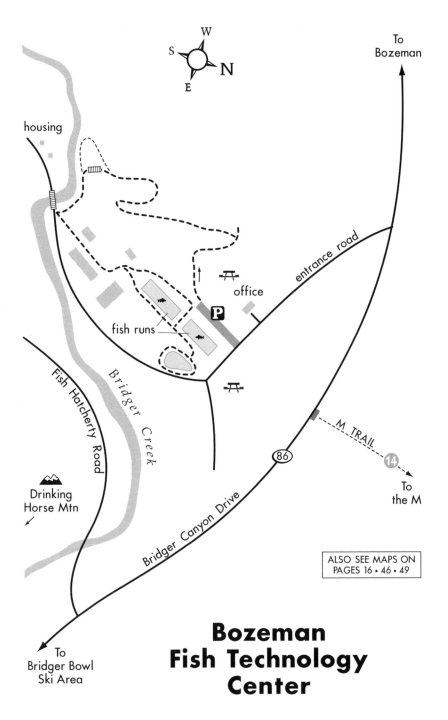

W
S · N
E

To
Bozeman

housing

entrance road

office

P

fish runs

Fish Hatcherly Road

Bridger Creek

Drinking
Horse Mtn

M TRAIL

86

14

To
the M

Bridger Canyon Drive

ALSO SEE MAPS ON
PAGES 16 • 46 • 49

To
Bridger Bowl
Ski Area

Bozeman
Fish Technology
Center

16. Cherry River Loop Trail
CHERRY RIVER FISHING ACCESS

Hiking distance: 0.8 mile loop
Hiking time: 30 minutes
Elevation gain: Level
Maps: U.S.G.S. Bozeman
      Gallatin Valley Land Trust map

map
page 56

Summary of hike: The Cherry River Fishing Access sits at the northwest corner of Bozeman along the East Gallatin River. The Cherry River, actually a portion of the East Gallatin River, was named in the early 1800s for its abundance of choke cherry trees. An interpretive trail loops through open grasslands and around the wetlands to the East Gallatin River. The Bridger Mountains serve as a backdrop to the beautiful preserve. Interpretive signs describe the riparian habitat, the birds, mammals, fish, and vegetation. The fishing access trails connect with Glen Lake in the East Gallatin Recreation Area (Hike 17) and continue to the Story Mill Trail (Hike 18), which are all part of the Main Street to the Mountains trail system.

Driving directions: From I-90 and the 7th Avenue overpass in Bozeman, drive 1 mile northbound on 7th Avenue (which becomes West Frontage Road) to the posted trailhead parking lot on the right.

Hiking directions: From the posted trailhead, take the left fork—the Cherry River Loop Trail. Pass interpretive signs while meandering clockwise toward the East Gallatin River. At the north end, curve right, passing a side path leading to the river. On the northeast corner of the main trail is a trail split. The left fork heads east through the grasslands and connects with the East Gallatin Trail at Glen Lake (Hike 17). Stay to the right along the east side of the wetland, passing cattails, willows, and dogwood. On the south side of the loop, skirt between both ponds on a raised berm, returning to the trailhead.

To extend the hike, head east from the southeast corner of the parking lot for 300 yards, connecting with the trail from the northeast corner of the loop by a footbridge. Continue one mile to the East Gallatin Recreation Area (Hikes 17—18).

17. Glen Lake to Cherry River
EAST GALLATIN RECREATION AREA to
CHERRY RIVER FISHING ACCESS

Hiking distance: 2.2 miles round trip
Hiking time: 1 hour
Elevation gain: 40 feet
Maps: U.S.G.S. Bozeman
      Gallatin Valley Land Trust map

**map
page 56**

Summary of hike: The East Gallatin River stretches about 25 miles northeast of Bozeman before joining the Gallatin River by the Horseshoe Hills out of Belgrade. This hike begins in the East Gallatin Recreation Area, an 83-acre park adjacent to the East Gallatin River at the northeast corner of Bozeman. The trail begins from Glen Lake and heads west to the Cherry River Fishing Access (Hike 16), also bordering the river.

Driving directions: From Main Street in downtown Bozeman, head north on North Rouse Avenue 1.4 miles to Griffin Drive. Turn left and drive 0.3 miles to Manley Road. Turn right and continue 0.6 miles to the signed East Gallatin Recreation Area. Turn right and drive 0.15 miles to the parking spaces on the left (just inside the fence) or 0.3 miles to the parking spaces on the right at the end of the road. All parking is on the east side of Glen Lake.

Hiking directions: Head west on the wide gravel path along the north side of Glen Lake to Manley Road. Cross the road and walk 100 yards down Gallatin Park Drive to the trail on the right, or walk 100 yards up Manley Road to the trail on the left. Both routes merge in a short distance and head west. Pass a pond on the right and skirt the base of the hill 50 feet below 7th Avenue. At a half mile, three hundred yards shy of the Cherry River Trailhead parking lot, is a posted junction by a footbridge. Bear right and cross the bridge over the stream. Walk north through the grasslands towards the Bridger Range. Before reaching the tree-lined East Gallatin River, curve left to a T-junction with the Cherry River Loop Trail (Hike 16). Both directions lead back to the trailhead. Pick up the trail on the southeast corner of the parking lot and head east, completing the loop. Return by retracing your route.

18. East Gallatin River Trail to Story Mill
EAST GALLATIN RECREATION AREA

Hiking distance: 2.2 miles round trip
Hiking time: 1 hour
Elevation gain: Level
Maps: U.S.G.S. Bozeman
      Gallatin Valley Land Trust map

map
next page

Summary of hike: The East Gallatin Recreation Area is an 83-acre park adjacent to the East Gallatin River at the northeast corner of Bozeman. The centerpiece of the park is Glen Lake (also referred to as East Gallatin Lake), developed over an old gravel pit. On the east side of the lake is Bozeman Beach, a 300-foot sandy beach strand. The popular lake is used for swimming, canoeing, kayaking, windsurfing, fishing, and sunbathing. Trails lead in both directions from the lake. To the west, the recreation area connects with the Cherry River Fishing Access (Hike 17). This hike leads east along the serpentine East Gallatin River, a popular bird-watching area, and crosses the river on a 70-foot bridge. Two loops wind through the riparian corridor and skirt the Bridger Creek Golf Course. The trails are part of the Main Street to the Mountains trail system, connecting with the Story Mill Trail (Hike 19).

Driving directions: Same as Hike 17.

Hiking directions: From Glen Lake, take either of the posted trails east. Both routes meet a short distance ahead in an open grassy meadow. Skirt the east edge of the meadow, bordering the lush vegetation that engulfs the river, to a signed junction at 0.3 miles. Straight ahead, the path follows the west edge of the river to the Rouse Avenue trailhead 0.3 miles ahead. Along the way, side paths lead to the riverbank. Bear left on the East Gallatin Connector Trail, and cross the East Gallatin Pedestrian Bridge, an arched metal bridge over the creek. At the T-junction, begin the loop on the right fork, following the river in a lush forest. Pass elbow bends in the river to a Y-fork. The main route goes left. For now go 12 yards to the right and another fork. This is a short loop through the forest and along the river. Return to the Y-fork and continue to another trail split. The left fork is our return route. Bear right and leave the forest, following the south edge of Bridger Creek Golf Course to Boylan Road. Curve right, staying on the footpath, with a view of the west flank of the Bridger Mountains. Head south, then east, passing homes and open grass-lands. Cross Birdie Drive and weave along the gravel path to the Story Mill Connector Trail. This is the turn-around spot. Return to the forested junction. Bear right and weave through the forest, crossing five bridges over the wetlands before completing the loop. Cross the bridge over the East Gallatin River to the right and retrace your steps.

For extended hiking, the trail connects to Hikes 17 and 19.

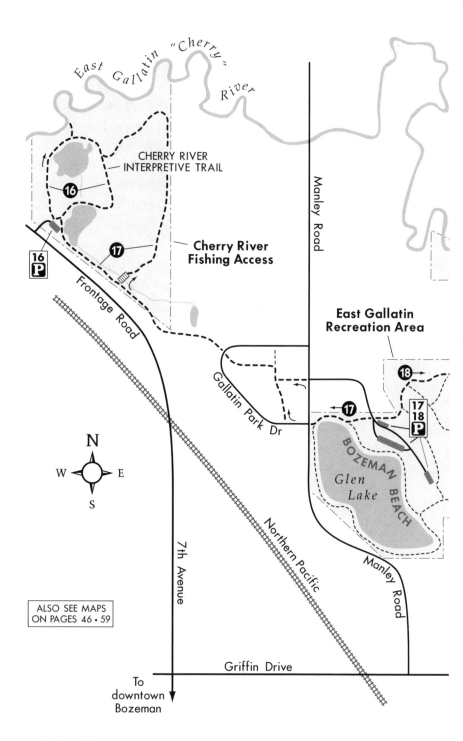

East Gallatin "Cherry" River

CHERRY RIVER
INTERPRETIVE TRAIL

16

17

**Cherry River
Fishing Access**

**16
P**

Frontage Road

Manley Road

**East Gallatin
Recreation Area**

18

Gallatin Park Dr

17

**17
18
P**

BOZEMAN BEACH

Glen
Lake

N

W · E

S

ALSO SEE MAPS
ON PAGES 46 · 59

7th Avenue

Northern Pacific

Manley Road

Griffin Drive

To
downtown
Bozeman

East Gallatin Recreation Area

HIKE 16
Cherry River Fishing Access

HIKE 17
Glen Lake to Cherry River

HIKE 18
East Gallatin River Trail

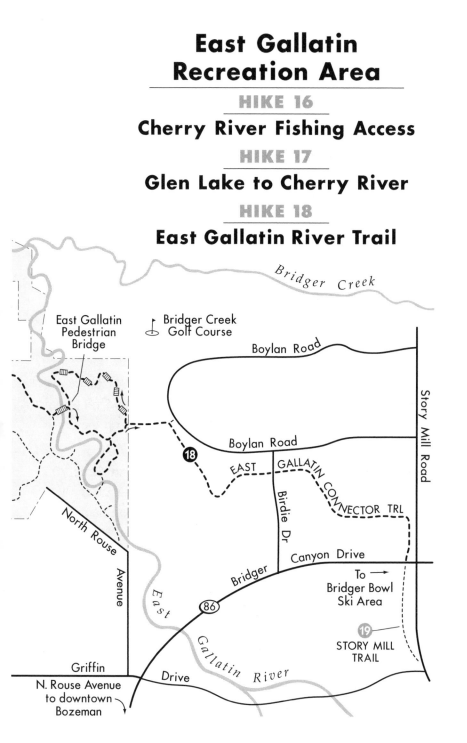

Bridger Creek

East Gallatin Pedestrian Bridge

Bridger Creek Golf Course

Boylan Road

Story Mill Road

Boylan Road

18

EAST GALLATIN CONNECTOR TRL

North Rouse Avenue

Birdie Dr

Canyon Drive

To → Bridger Bowl Ski Area

Bridger

86

East

19
STORY MILL TRAIL

Griffin

Gallatin River

Drive

N. Rouse Avenue to downtown Bozeman

19. Story Mill Spur Trail

Hiking distance: 2 miles round trip
Hiking time: 1 hour
Elevation gain: Level
Maps: U.S.G.S. Bozeman

Summary of hike: Back in 1883, Story Mill was the largest flour mill in Montana. It was also the first business in Bozeman serviced by the railroad. Railroad tracks, known as the Story Mill Spur, lead 4,400 feet to the historic mill. The Story Mill Spur Trail is an interpretive trail along the railroad right-of-way. The trail crosses the East Gallatin River, where benches have been placed in the shade of the cottonwood trees. The hike continues past the Bozeman Livestock yards and the historic Story Mill to Bridger Canyon Drive, where it now connects to the East Gallatin River Trail (Hike 18). The Gallatin Valley Land Trust worked 9 years to make this historic trail into a reality.

Driving directions: From Main Street in downtown Bozeman, take North Wallace Street 0.6 miles to East Tamarack Street. Turn right and park alongside the road. The trail begins on the north side of the railroad tracks.

Hiking directions: Walk north on North Wallace Street 0.1 mile, crossing the railroad tracks to the signed trail on the left side of the road. Take the trail along the right side of the railroad tracks heading north. Cross over the tracks and under I-90. The trail narrows and the shrub-lined path heads directly towards the Bridger Mountains. Continue past farmhouses, barns, and horses. Cross a wooden footbridge over the East Gallatin River, and pass the cottonwood grove by the historic remains of the Gallatin Valley Auction Yard. The trail connects with the unpaved Story Mill Road. Bear left past the mills to the signed footpath on the left side of the road. The trail ends at Bridger Drive. To extend the hike, cross Bridger Drive and follow the Story Mill Connector Trail along the west side of Story Mill Road.

A short distance ahead is a posted junction with the East Gallatin Connector Trail leading to Glen Lake at the East Gallatin Recreation Area (Hike 18).

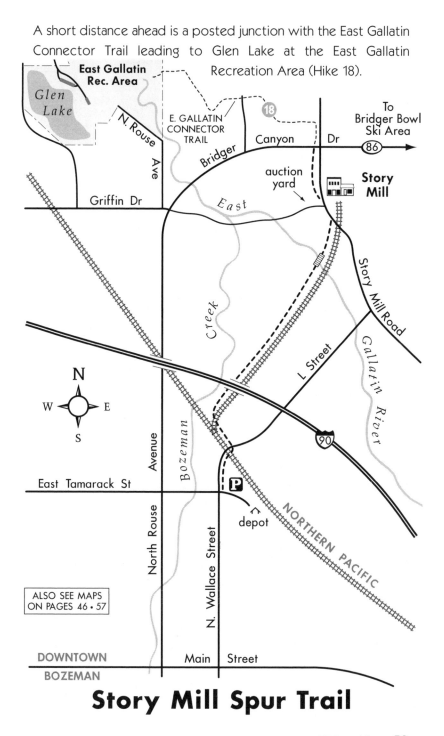

ALSO SEE MAPS
ON PAGES 46 · 57

Story Mill Spur Trail

20. Gallagator Trail
TO MUSEUM OF THE ROCKIES

Hiking distance: 2.2 miles round trip
Hiking time: 1 hour
Elevation gain: Level
Maps: U.S.G.S. Bozeman
Gallatin Valley Land Trust map

map
next page

Summary of hike: The Gallagator Trail follows the route of the old Milwaukee Road railroad track, which took passengers between Bozeman and the Gallatin Gateway. The route was abandoned in the late 1930s. The right-of-way is now a Main Street to the Mountains hiking and biking trail that begins at the base of Peets Hill by Burke Park. The path crosses several bridges over Bozeman (Sourdough) Creek and Mathew Bird Creek, ending at a picnic area by the Museum of the Rockies. En route, a spur trail leads through Langhor Park. There are several street crossings along the route.

Driving directions: From Main Street at the east end of downtown Bozeman, drive south on South Church Avenue 0.4 miles to the parking area on the left, across from Story Street at the base of Peets Hill.

Hiking directions: Cross South Church Avenue to the corner of Story Street. Take the signed trail southwest along Gallagator Linear Park. Follow the wide, tree-lined path along an old railroad right-of-way. Cross a wooden bridge over Bozeman Creek. At 0.2 miles, cross a second bridge over Mathew Bird Creek to a junction. The side path on the right leads to a fork. The right fork goes through an aspen grove and exits by Anderson Street, just east of Black Avenue. The left fork loops back to the main trail. Continue along Mathew Bird Creek past scenic backyards. Pass a bridge on the right that crosses over the creek to the south end of Black Avenue. Cross another bridge over Mathew Bird Creek at a half mile, 30 yards shy of Garfield Street After crossing the road, follow the trail along the right side of the creek to the signed Langhor Spur Trail on the left. The spur trail leads through the streamside park on the west side of the waterway to Langhor Gardens at Mason Street and Tracy Avenue. En route, the spur passes a climbing rock on the left and a trail that crosses a bridge over the creek to Tracy Avenue. On the main trail, continue southwest, passing a pond on the left to South Willson Avenue. Cross the road and bear left 70 yards to Lincoln Street. Pick up the path again by the wooden trail posts on the southwest corner. Follow the hedge-lined path to Kagy Boulevard. Cross the road to the Museum of the Rockies. Follow the path to a picnic area by the metal horse sculpture. To return, retrace your steps.

21. Chris Boyd—Highland Ridge Trail

Hiking distance: 4.4 miles round trip
Hiking time: 2 hours
Elevation gain: 100 feet
Maps: U.S.G.S. Bozeman
Gallatin Valley Land Trust map

**map
next page**

Summary of hike: Burke Park is a 42-acre linear park that parallels South Church Avenue. It is the hub of the Main Street to the Mountains trail system. Highland Ridge is a low 100-foot bluff that runs above South Church Avenue the length of the park. The Highland Ridge Trail begins at Peets Hill in Burke Park and heads south along the ridge to the city water tower. From the top of the hill are views across Bozeman to the Bridger, Gallatin, and Madison Ranges. Benches are placed along the ridge for savoring the views, which include the Bozeman Creek corridor. The first segment of the trail has been renamed and dedicated to Chris Boyd, founder of the Gallatin Valley Land Trust. Beyond the ridge, the path skirts the edge of a subdivision and meanders through rolling grasslands, connecting with the Painted Hills Trail (Hike 22).

Driving directions: Same as Hike 20.

Hiking directions: Walk 20 yards up the posted path to a trail split and map kiosk in Burke Park. The left fork climbs to Lindley Park. Bear right and head up Peets Hill to the ridge. From the top are several paths. Take the Chris Boyd Trail, which begins in Lindley Park, and head south. Follow the hillside ridge through Burke Park. Pass the Wortman Spur Trail on the right that leads down the hillside to Church Avenue.

New Hyalite View Subdivision

㉑ HIGHLAND RIDGE

Continue along the ridge 0.7 miles to a signed junction with the Simkins Spur Trail at the water tower. Bear left on the Highland Ridge Trail. Follow the wooden rail fence to the east to Highland Boulevard, between farmland to the north and a row of homes to the south. Go to the left 75 yards on the paved bike path and cross the road, picking up the signed trail again. The path curves around the perimeter of New Hyalite View subdivision and curves south through the rolling grasslands. At 2.3 miles, the trail forks. Curve left, reaching Kagy Boulevard. Follow the Kagy Connector Trail east, crossing the road to the Painted Hills Trailhead 0.4 miles ahead (Hike 22). Continue with the next hike, or return on the same path.

Highland Blvd

HIKE 20
Gallagator Trail
HIKE 21
Chris Boyd– Highland Ridge Trail

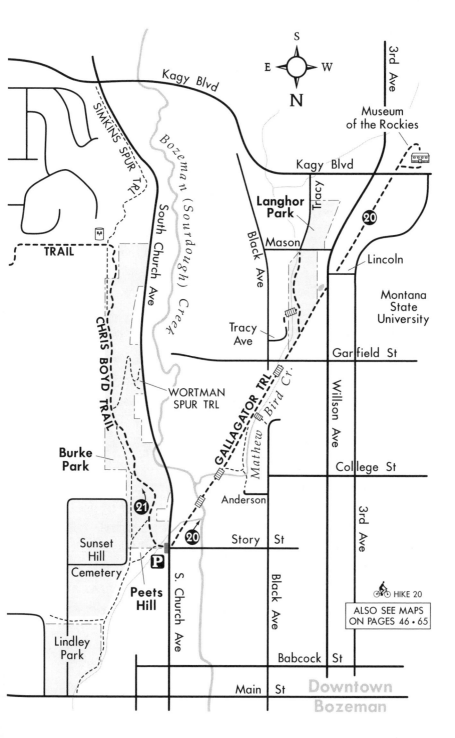

Kagy Blvd

S
E — W
N

SIMKINS SPUR TRL

3rd Ave

Museum
of the Rockies

Kagy Blvd

Bozeman (Sourdough) Creek

Langhor
Park

Tracy

20

Mason

Black Ave

Lincoln

TRAIL

South Church Ave

Montana
State
University

CHRIS BOYD TRAIL

Tracy
Ave

Garfield St

Matthew Bird Cr.

GALLAGATOR TRL.

WORTMAN
SPUR TRL

Willson Ave

College St

Burke
Park

Anderson

3rd Ave

21

20

Story St

Sunset
Hill

Peets
Hill

S. Church Ave

Black Ave

Cemetery

🚲 HIKE 20

ALSO SEE MAPS
ON PAGES 46 • 65

Lindley
Park

Babcock St

Main St

Downtown
Bozeman

22. Painted Hills Trail

Hiking distance: 2.5 miles round trip
Hiking time: 1 hour
Elevation gain: Level
Maps: U.S.G.S. Bozeman
Gallatin Valley Land Trust map

Summary of hike: The Painted Hills are tucked into the southeast corner of Gallatin Valley and Bozeman, just north of Mount Ellis. The Painted Hills Trail begins near the south end of the Highland Ridge Trail (Hike 21). (The Kagy Connector Trail links these two trails together.) The trail passes through dedicated parkland along a gully near the Painted Hills subdivision. The path heads south, crossing a small stream, and currently ends at a private property fenceline. The Gallatin Valley Land Trust is actively working to connect it with the Triple Tree Trail (Hike 23).

Driving directions: From Main Street at the east end of downtown Bozeman, drive south on South Church Avenue 1.6 miles to Kagy Boulevard. (South Church Avenue becomes Sourdough Road after Kagy Boulevard.) Turn left on Kagy Boulevard, and drive 0.9 miles to the trailhead parking area on the right.

Hiking directions: Head south past the trail sign, following the east edge of the draw. Continue across a series of small rises and dips. Cross a wooden footbridge over a seasonal drainage. At 0.6 miles, cross McGee Drive in the Painted Hills subdivision. Pick up the trail again and cross another footbridge. Bear left on the narrow footpath and continue up the draw. The trail currently ends at 1.25 miles at a private property fence. Return by retracing your steps.

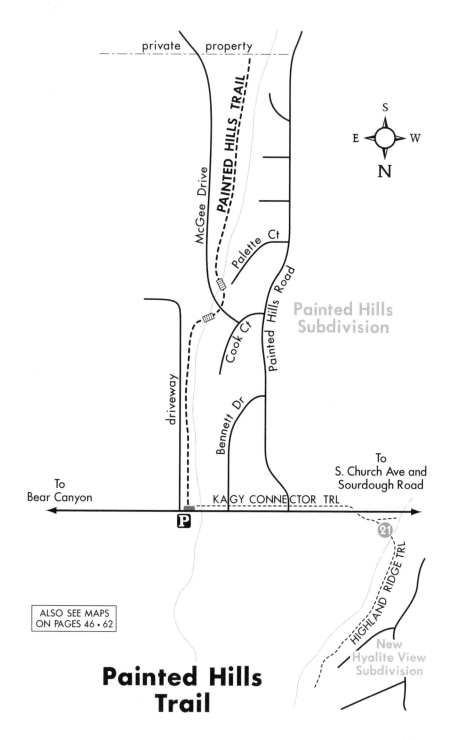

private property

PAINTED HILLS TRAIL

McGee Drive

Palette Ct

Painted Hills Road

Painted Hills Subdivision

Cook Ct

Bennett Dr

driveway

To
Bear Canyon

KAGY CONNECTOR TRL

P

To
S. Church Ave and
Sourdough Road

21

HIGHLAND RIDGE TRL

New
Hyalite View
Subdivision

ALSO SEE MAPS
ON PAGES 46 • 62

S
E — W
N

Painted Hills
Trail

23. Triple Tree Trail

Hiking distance: 4.5 miles round trip
Hiking time: 2 hours
Elevation gain: 800 feet
Maps: U.S.G.S. Wheeler Mountain and Mount Ellis
Gallatin Valley Land Trust map

Summary of hike: The Triple Tree Trail is on the southeast corner of Gallatin Valley, south of Bozeman. It begins on a grassy ridge, crosses Limestone Creek, and loops through the northwest slope of Mount Ellis on Montana state land. The trail weaves through shaded woodlands to a hilltop knoll in a wildflower-covered meadow. From the summit are 360-degree views of Gallatin Valley and the Gallatin, Madison, Tobacco Root, and Bridger Ranges.

Driving directions: From Main Street in downtown Bozeman, drive south on South Church Avenue 4.6 miles to the signed parking lot on the left. The parking lot is 200 feet south of Triple Tree Road. (South Church Avenue becomes Sourdough Road after Kagy Boulevard.)

Hiking directions: Follow the wide grassy path east past the trailhead sign, and cross the rolling slopes. Enter an aspen grove and cross two footbridges over Limestone Creek. Emerge from the forest into the open meadow, and climb the slope to a signed junction at one mile. The left fork continues across the grasslands and crosses several subdivision roads. Take the right fork and follow the buck fence down into the drainage. Cross the bridge over Limestone Creek and another bridge over the wetlands. Ascend the hill into the forest to a trail split at 1.5 miles. Take the right fork, beginning the loop, and head up the west side of the draw into state land. Bear sharply to the right, and climb up the hillside. Follow the ridge up a winding course. At the top is a meadow with fantastic vistas. After enjoying the views, cross the meadow and begin the descent into the forested drainage.

Head down the draw along the right side of a trickling stream. Near the bottom, cross the stream, completing the loop. Retrace your steps to return.

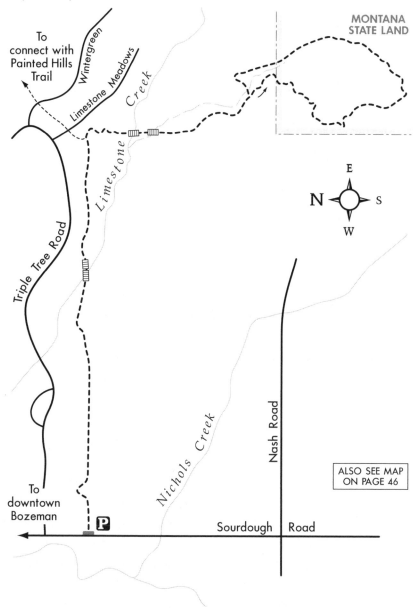

Triple Tree Trail

24. Sourdough Trail

Hiking distance: 3.2 miles round trip
Hiking time: 1.5 hours
Elevation gain: 100 feet
Maps: U.S.G.S. Bozeman
      Gallatin Valley Land Trust map

map next page

Summary of hike: Bozeman (Sourdough) Creek begins in Mystic Lake on the southeast flank of Mount Ellis. The creek, Bozeman's only major stream corridor, threads its way through the city en route to the East Gallatin River. The Sourdough Trail follows a portion of Bozeman Creek under the shade of aspen and cottonwoods. After several creek crossings, the path breaks out into the grassy meadows, skirts the Valley View Golf Course, and meanders through Graf Park. In the winter, the Sourdough Trail is a popular cross-country ski trail.

Driving directions: From Main Street in downtown Bozeman, drive south on South Church Avenue 3.1 miles to Goldenstein Lane. It is 1.5 miles south of Kagy Boulevard. (En route, South Church Avenue becomes Sourdough Road.) Turn right on Goldenstein Lane, and drive 0.5 miles to the posted trailhead parking area on the right, 100 yards after crossing Bozeman Creek.

Hiking directions: Walk 100 yards east on the Goldenstein Trail, paralleling Goldenstein Lane to Bozeman Creek. Curve left and head north on the forested path downstream along the west edge of the creek. Short side paths lead to the creek bank. Wind through the shaded forest to a posted trail split at a half mile. Detour right, crossing a 60-foot arching metal bridge over the creek in Gardner Park. On the upstream side of the bridge is a pool in the creek. Return to the main trail, and cross over a stream to a junction with the Sundance Trail on the left (Hike 25). Continue straight, staying on the forested Sourdough Trail. Cross a bridge over Nash-Spring Creek, and follow the creek to the fenced Valley View Golf Course. Curve left, skirting the edge of the golf course to Graf Street, just south of Spring Meadow Drive. Go to the right, picking up the signed footpath at Graf Park on the right. Walk through the parkland meadow on the east side of aspen-lined Mathew Bird Creek. The trail ends on Fairway Drive between homes.

25. Sundance Trail Loop

Hiking distance: 2.5 mile loop
Hiking time: 1.5 hours
Elevation gain: Level
Maps: U.S.G.S. Bozeman
  Gallatin Valley Land Trust map

map
next page

Summary of hike: The Sundance subdivision sits on the south side of Bozeman between 3rd Avenue and Goldenstein Lane. The first half mile of this loop hike follows the forested Sourdough Trail (Hike 24) along Bozeman Creek. It then leaves the forest and weaves through the open grasslands preserved within the subdivision, crossing bridges over Nash-Spring Creek and Mathew Bird Creek.

Driving directions: From Main Street in downtown Bozeman, drive south on South Church Avenue 3.1 miles to Goldenstein Lane. It is 1.5 miles south of Kagy Boulevard. (En route, South Church Avenue becomes Sourdough Road.) Turn right on Goldenstein Lane, and drive 0.5 miles to the posted trailhead parking area on the right, 100 yards after crossing Bozeman Creek.

Hiking directions: Walk 100 yards east on the Goldenstein Trail, paralleling Goldenstein Lane to Bozeman Creek. Curve left and head north on the forested path downstream along the west edge of the creek. Short side paths lead to the creek bank. Wind through the shaded forest to a posted trail split at a half mile. Detour right, crossing a 60-foot arching metal bridge over the creek in Gardner Park. On the upstream side of the bridge is a pool in the creek. Return to the main trail, and cross over a stream to a junction with the Sundance Trail on the left. The Sourdough Trail (Hike 24) continues straight. Bear left and cross a bridge over serpentine Nash-Spring Creek. Meander through the open grasslands in the Sundance subdivision and cross Graf Street. Weave to a junction, located just after crossing a bridge over Mathew Bird Creek. The right fork leads to a trailhead at the end of Sundance Drive. Stay to the left and parallel an irrigation ditch to another junction. The trail straight ahead ends at Peace Pipe Drive. Bear right on the McCloud Park Trail, and stroll through the meadow to 3rd Avenue. Curve left, parallel the road, and cross Little Horse Drive to Goldenstein Lane. Head east on the path along Goldenstein Lane for 0.2 miles, where the path ends. Walk 0.3 miles along the road, and return to the trail and the trailhead.

HIKE 24

Sourdough Trail

HIKE 25

Sundance Trail Loop

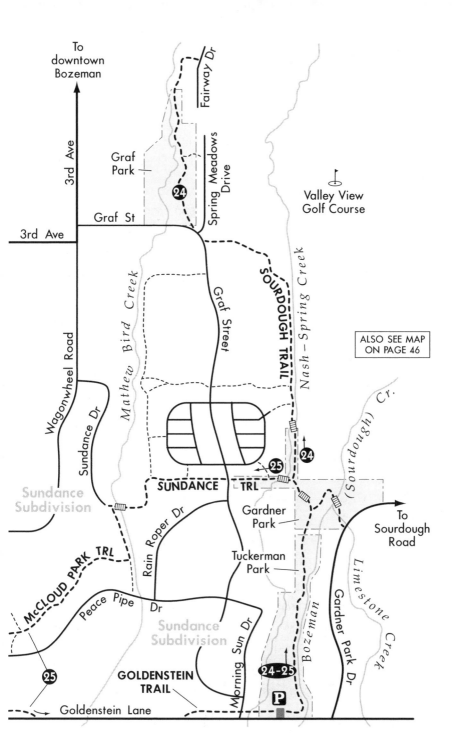

To
downtown
Bozeman

3rd Ave

Graf
Park

Graf St

3rd Ave

Fairway Dr

Spring Meadows Drive

24

Valley View
Golf Course

Wagonwheel Road

Mathew Bird Creek

Sundance Dr

Graf Street

SOURDOUGH TRAIL

Nash–Spring Creek

ALSO SEE MAP
ON PAGE 46

Sundance
Subdivision

24

25

SUNDANCE TRL

Gardner
Park

Rain Roper Dr

(Sourdough) Cr.

To
Sourdough
Road

McCLOUD PARK TRL

Peace Pipe Dr

Tuckerman
Park

Sundance
Subdivision

Morning Sun Dr

Limestone Creek

Bozeman

Gardner Park Dr

25

GOLDENSTEIN
TRAIL

24-25

P

Goldenstein Lane

26. Lower Mount Ellis

Hiking distance: 6 miles round trip
Hiking time: 3.5 hours
Elevation gain: 2,400 feet
Maps: U.S.G.S. Kelly Creek and Mount Ellis
    Beartooth Publishing: Bozeman, Big Sky, W. Yellowstone

map
next page

Summary of hike: Mount Ellis lies on the southeast edge of Bozeman at the north end of the Gallatin Range, between New World Gulch and Bozeman Creek Canyon. The mountain has two peaks, with the higher 8,331-foot peak to the south. A long sweeping saddle connects the two summits. This hike climbs up the northeast slope of Mount Ellis to the lower 7,690-foot peak. Atop the lower peak is a clearing with Madison limestone outcroppings and gorgeous vistas.

Driving directions: From Bozeman, drive east on I-90 to the Bear Canyon Road exit, the first exit east of Bozeman. Turn right on Bozeman Trail Road, and continue 0.7 miles to Mount Ellis Lane. Turn left and drive 1.75 miles to the end of the public road by private property gates. Park on the right side of the road.

From Kagy Boulevard and Sourdough Road in Bozeman, drive 3.5 miles east on Kagy Boulevard to Mount Ellis Lane, across from a large, old barn. (En route, Kagy Boulevard becomes Bozeman Trail Road.) Turn right and continue 1.75 miles to the end of the public road by private property gates.

Hiking directions: Pass through the wooden state land gate. Follow the old jeep road on an upward slope through the open pastureland. Head toward the treeline at the base of prominent Mount Ellis. Along the way are sweeping vistas across the Gallatin Valley to the Bangtail, Bridger, and Tobacco Root Mountains. At one mile, enter the shade of an aspen and pine forest. Pass a wide, grassy path on the right that leads to Limestone Creek, and continue 70 yards to a cattle gate. Climb the west wall of the canyon and curve left, looping out of the draw. Traverse the north face of Mount Ellis through lodgepole pines, curving around a second drainage. At 2 miles, the old road tops out on an open flat with a trail split. To the left, the grassy path descends into New World Gulch (Hike 27). One hundred yards along this route is an overlook into the canyon. (Continuing into the gulch, this path becomes vague and is hard to follow.) Back on the main trail, continue up the right (west) fork, and make a horseshoe bend through the old logging area. Make a sweeping left bend and head south, with views of Upper Mount Ellis and Bozeman Creek Canyon. Make another U-shaped bend to views of Bozeman and the Gallatin Valley. A footpath veers to the right and leads to the old-growth forest. Steeply climb to the summit of Lower Mount Ellis.

To extend the hike, a path follows the ridge across the sweeping saddle 1.4 miles, climbing nearly 1,000 feet to the upper peak.

27. New World Gulch Trail

Hiking distance: 4.4 miles round trip
Hiking time: 2.5 hours
Elevation gain: 1,000 feet

map
next page

Maps: U.S.G.S. Mount Ellis
   Beartooth Publishing: Bozeman, Big Sky, W. Yellowstone
   U.S.F.S. Gallatin National Forest: West Half or East Half

Summary of hike: New World Gulch is located southeast of Bozeman between Bear Canyon and the east slope of Mount Ellis. The stream-fed gulch, due north of Mystic Lake, is a tributary of Bear Creek. The New World Gulch Trail climbs the divide between New World Gulch and the Bozeman Creek drainage for 4.7 miles, ending at Mystic Lake. This hike heads up the narrow drainage 2.2 miles to a meadow and canyon. The area retains water, which causes muddy spots along the trail early in the season. The trail is part of a 5.5-mile loop, although the adjoining loop trail is diffi-cult to find. This hike returns along the same trail.

Driving directions: From Bozeman, drive east on I-90 to the Bear Canyon Road exit, the first exit east of Bozeman. Turn right on Bozeman Trail Road, and continue 0.2 miles to Bear Canyon Road. Turn left and drive 3.4 miles to the trailhead parking area on the right.

From Kagy Boulevard and Sourdough Road in Bozeman, drive 4 miles east on Kagy Boulevard to Bear Canyon Road. (En route, Kagy Boulevard becomes Bozeman Trail Road.) Turn right continue 3.4 miles to the parking area on the right.

Hiking directions: Hike south past the buck fence, and climb up the hill. Follow the forested path and cross several streams. After crossing New World Creek on a rickety wooden bridge, enter a lodgepole pine forest, where the elevation gain increases. At 1.9 miles, descend to the gulch and a drainage stream. From the stream, detour on the faint trail downstream 400 yards to a beautiful, lush canyon with small waterfalls and ferns. Return to the main trail, and continue upstream 0.2 miles to a large meadow. This is our turn-around spot. To return, retrace your steps. Beyond the meadow, the trail continues on to Mystic Lake 2.5 miles farther.

To make a loop, a faint trail leads west from the meadow across the stream. Once across, the seldom used trail (known by bikers as the Skin In Trail) is a scramble to find.

Francham
Mountain
7,130'

BEAR CYN
28
BEAR TRL

HIKE 26
Lower Mount Ellis

HIKE 27
New World Gulch

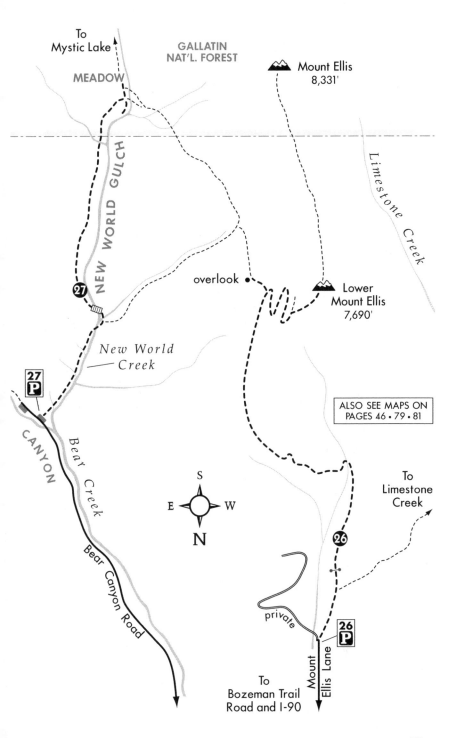

To
Mystic Lake

GALLATIN
NAT'L. FOREST

MEADOW

Mount Ellis
8,331'

NEW WORLD GULCH

27

Limestone Creek

overlook •

Lower
Mount Ellis
7,690'

New World
— Creek

27 P

CANYON

Bear Creek

ALSO SEE MAPS ON
PAGES 46 • 79 • 81

To
Limestone
Creek

S
E — W
N

26

Bear Canyon Road

private

26 P

Mount Ellis Lane

To
Bozeman Trail
Road and I-90

28. Bear Canyon Trail

Hiking distance: 4.4 miles round trip
Hiking time: 2.5 hours
Elevation gain: 400 feet
Maps: U.S.G.S. Mount Ellis and Bald Knob

Beartooth Publishing: Bozeman, Big Sky, W. Yellowstone
U.S.F.S. Gallatin National Forest: West Half or East Half

Summary of hike: Bear Canyon is a stream-fed canyon south-east of Bozeman between Mount Ellis, Francham Mountain, and Chestnut Mountain. Bear Creek forms on the upper north slope of Bald Knob and flows through the canyon to the East Gallatin River. The Bear Canyon Trail follows Bear Creek five miles up the lush, shady canyon to the Bear Lakes. This hike takes in the first 2.2 miles of the trail, which includes several creek crossings and a one-mile loop. The trail stays close to the cascading waters of the creek. Beyond this hike, the Bear Canyon Trail climbs 1,400 feet to the Bear Lakes, which sit on a flat at 6,900 feet. (En route to the lakes is the trail to Chestnut Mountain—Hike 29.)

Driving directions: From Bozeman, drive east on I-90 to the Bear Canyon Road exit, the first exit east of Bozeman. Turn right on Bozeman Trail Road, and continue 0.2 miles to Bear Canyon Road. Turn left and drive 3.5 miles to the trailhead parking area on the left at the end of the road.

From Kagy Boulevard and Sourdough Road in Bozeman, drive 4 miles east on Kagy Boulevard to Bear Canyon Road. (En route, Kagy Boulevard becomes Bozeman Trail Road.) Turn right continue 3.5 miles to the trailhead parking area on the left at the end of the road.

Hiking directions: Head southeast on the old jeep road, parallel to the southwest side of Bear Creek. Traverse the canyon wall through the lush forest above the creek. The trail runs beneath the weathered sandstone formations on Francham Mountain. Rock-hop over Bear Creek two successive times as the canyon narrows. Pass through a trail gate at the Gallatin National Forest boundary. Cross the mouth of stream-fed Shoefelt Gulch, where a side path veers right into the side canyon. Cross to the north side of Bear Creek and pass Dean Gulch, where another side path curves left into the draw. Continue straight to a posted junction, located just after crossing a culvert over Bear Creek. Begin the loop on the right fork and descend to the creek. Cross a wooden bridge over the creek to a grassy meadow beneath Chestnut Mountain at 2.2 miles. Two hundred feet ahead is a junction. The main trail continues through the meadow to the right and leads 3 miles to the Bear Lakes. Take the left fork and walk downstream, meandering through the rolling, tree-filled meadow. Cross the creek and complete the loop. Retrace your steps to the right.

29. Bear Canyon Trail to Chestnut Mountain

Hiking distance: 10 miles round trip
Hiking time: 5 hours
Elevation gain: 2,100 feet
Maps: U.S.G.S. Mount Ellis and Bald Knob
Beartooth Publishing: Bozeman, Big Sky, W. Yellowstone
U.S.F.S. Gallatin National Forest: West Half or East Half

map
next page

Summary of hike: Chestnut Mountain sits on the northeast tip of the Gallatin Range a few miles east of Bozeman. The 7,615-foot mountain rises between Mount Ellis and Bozeman Pass. Bear Canyon sits at the west foot of Chestnut Mountain and provides the easiest access to the ridge. This hike follows Bear Creek, then weaves through grassy meadows with historic log cabins. The trail ascends Chestnut Mountain from its southern end and follows the ridge to panoramic vistas of the surrounding peaks and mountain ranges.

Driving directions: Same as Hike 28.

Hiking directions: Pass the gate and traverse the southwest canyon wall in a lush forest. The trail runs beneath the weathered sandstone formations on Francham Mountain. Parallel Bear Creek on the left, and rock-hop over the creek two successive times as the canyon narrows. Pass through a trail gate at the Gallatin National Forest boundary. Cross the mouth of stream-fed Shoefelt Gulch, where a side path veers right into the side canyon. Cross to the north side of Bear Creek and pass Dean Gulch, where another side path curves left into the draw. Stay on the main trail to a posted junction, just after crossing a culvert over Bear Creek. Continue straight and descend to the creek. Cross the creek on a wooden bridge to a grassy meadow beneath Chestnut Mountain at 2.2 miles. To the left is the return loop for Hike 29. Go right (southeast), and stroll through the meadows. Climb through pine groves with intermittent views of Bald Knob. Walk through another huge meadow with an old log cabin and two sheds on the right. Another cabin sits at the far north end of the meadow. Steeply climb out of the meadow (passing the faint continuation of the Bear Creek Trail on the right) to a flat ridge and a Y-fork. The right fork leads one mile to logging roads. Bear left and climb to the south end of Chestnut Mountain. Climb the grassy ridge northwest to 360-degree views that include Bear Canyon; Bare Knob; Mount Ellis; and the Absaroka, Crazy, Bangtail, and Bridger Mountains. Continue up the spine to the tree-dotted summit. Follow the ridge over minor ups and downs, choosing your own turn-around spot.

HIKE 28
Bear Canyon Trail Loop

HIKE 29
Bear Canyon Trail to Chestnut Mountain

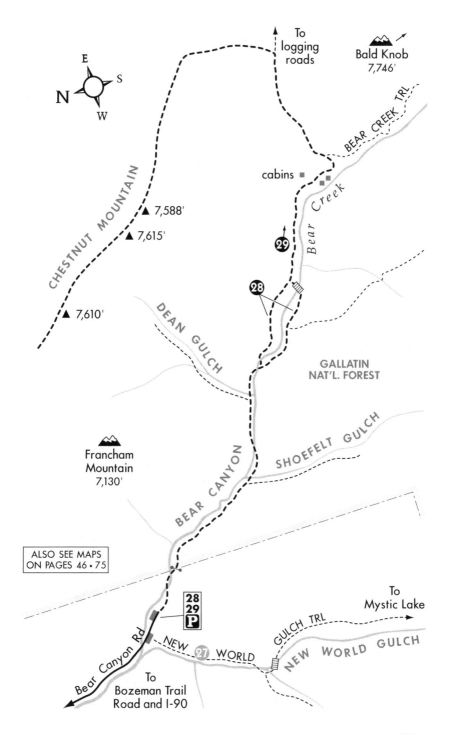

To logging roads

Bald Knob
7,746'

N E S W

BEAR CREEK TRL.

cabins

Bear Creek

CHESTNUT MOUNTAIN

▲ 7,588'

▲ 7,615'

▲ 7,610'

29

28

DEAN GULCH

GALLATIN NAT'L. FOREST

Francham Mountain
7,130'

BEAR CANYON

SHOEFELT GULCH

ALSO SEE MAPS ON PAGES 46 • 75

To Mystic Lake

28
29
P

GULCH TRL.

NEW WORLD

27

NEW WORLD GULCH

Bear Canyon Rd

To Bozeman Trail Road and I-90

30. Sourdough Canyon Road

Hiking distance: 0.5 to 16 miles round trip (to Mystic Lake)
Hiking time: 30 minutes to 9 hours
Elevation gain: Approximately 200 feet per mile
Maps: U.S.G.S. Wheeler Mountain and Mount Ellis
Crystal Bench Maps: Bozeman, Montana

Summary of hike: The headwaters of Bozeman (Sourdough) Creek flow from Mystic Lake and the east slope of Palisade Mountain. The creek, a major source of water for the city of Bozeman, weaves through the city en route to the East Gallatin River. The Sourdough Canyon Road is an old logging road. It parallels Bozeman Creek for 8 miles through a pine, fir, and spruce forest from the mouth of Sourdough Canyon to Mystic Lake. The close proximity to town and easy grade makes this a popular hiking, biking, equestrian, and cross-country skiing route.

Driving directions: From the east end of downtown Bozeman, drive south on South Church Avenue 5.2 miles to Nash Road. (South Church Avenue becomes Sourdough Road after Kagy Boulevard.) Turn right on Nash Road, and continue 0.2 miles to Sourdough Canyon Road on the left. Turn left and drive 0.9 miles to the trailhead parking area at road's end.

Hiking directions: Pass the trailhead gate and head southeast along the wide, forested road. Parallel Bozeman Creek through Sourdough Canyon at a steady but gradual uphill grade. At 4.7 miles is a junction and a bridge crossing over the creek. The Mystic Lake Trail (known locally as the Wall of Death) stays on the northwest side of the creek and continues 3 miles to the south end of Mystic Lake. The road (to the right) crosses over the bridge to a junction. The right fork climbs to Moser Creek Road and descends to Langhor Campground (Hikes 35 and 36). The left fork leads to Mystic Lake and to the Wild Horse Trail, which drops downhill to the Hyalite Reservoir (Hike 38). Choose your own turn-around spot.

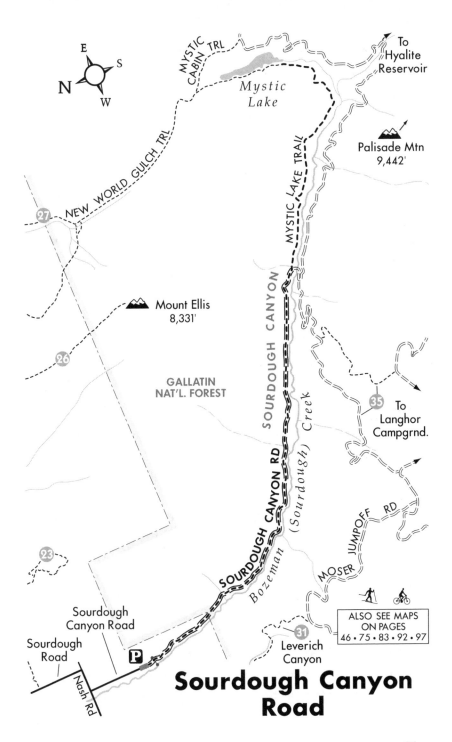

To
Hyalite
Reservoir

MYSTIC CABIN TRL

Mystic
Lake

Palisade Mtn
9,442'

MYSTIC LAKE TRAIL

NEW WORLD GULCH TRL

27

SOURDOUGH CANYON

Mount Ellis
8,331'

26

GALLATIN
NAT'L. FOREST

(Sourdough) Creek

35

To
Langhor
Campgrnd.

JUMPOFF RD

MOSER

23

SOURDOUGH CANYON RD

Bozeman

31

Sourdough
Canyon Road

Leverich
Canyon

Sourdough
Road

Nash Rd

P

ALSO SEE MAPS
ON PAGES
46 • 75 • 83 • 92 • 97

Sourdough Canyon
Road

31. Leverich Canyon Trail

Hiking distance: 3.4 miles round trip
Hiking time: 2 hours
Elevation gain: 1,100 feet
Maps: U.S.G.S. Wheeler Mountain

Summary of hike: Leverich Canyon is a beautiful, narrow canyon south of Bozeman, tucked between Sourdough Canyon and Hyalite Canyon. The trail follows Leverich Creek for the first half of the hike to an old miner's cabin, then climbs to the head of the canyon. From the top are great views of Bozeman, Sourdough Canyon, and the Bridger Mountains.

Driving directions: From Main Street at the west end of Bozeman, drive south on 19th Avenue for 5 miles to Nash Road. Turn left and drive 0.4 miles to South Third Road. Turn right and continue one mile to the end of the pavement. Follow the narrow unpaved lane straight ahead for one mile to the trailhead parking lot. At 0.8 miles, road moguls may make driving difficult. If so, park and walk 0.2 miles up the road.

Hiking directions: Take the footpath heading south from the south end of the parking area. Immediately cross Leverich Creek three times. Follow the narrow canyon uphill along the watercourse. At 0.8 miles cross Leverich Creek to the left and head uphill, away from the creek. At 0.9 miles is a sharp right bend in the trail. On the right side of the bend is a mine and an old log cabin. The trail becomes steeper and corkscrews its way up the mountain. Near the top, the path levels out and traverses the mountainside 1,400 feet above Bozeman Creek. The trail ends at a junction with the Moser Jumpoff Road, a gravel logging road. Return back down the canyon.

To extend the hike, the left fork leads to Bozeman Creek Road (Hike 30) and Langhor Campground in Hyalite Canyon (Hikes 35 and 36). The right fork connects with Kirk Hill (Hikes 32 and 33).

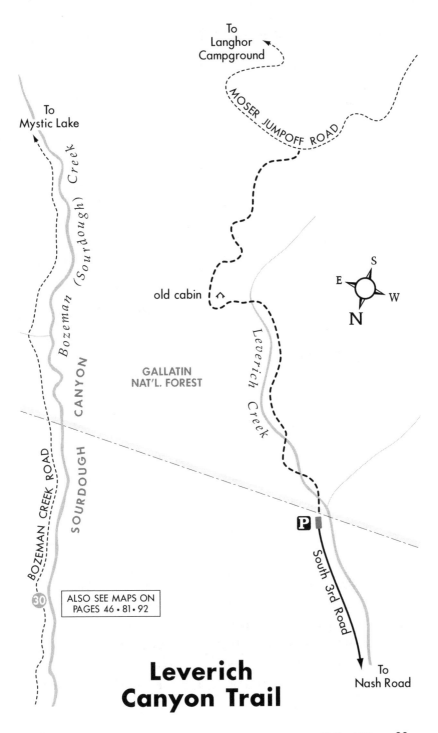

To
Langhor
Campground

To
Mystic Lake

MOSER JUMPOFF ROAD

Bozeman (Sourdough) Creek

old cabin

GALLATIN
NAT'L. FOREST

Leverich Creek

S

E   W

N

CANYON

SOURDOUGH

BOZEMAN CREEK ROAD

30

ALSO SEE MAPS ON
PAGES 46 • 81 • 92

P

South 3rd Road

To
Nash Road

Leverich
Canyon Trail

32. Kirk Hill (LOOPS 1 · 3)

Hiking distance: 1.7 miles round trip
Hiking time: 45 minutes
Elevation gain: 600 feet
Maps: U.S.G.S. Wheeler Mountain
　　　　Kirk Hill Nature Trail Map

**map
page 86**

Summary of hike: Kirk Hill is an open space with a triple loop trail in the northern foothills of the Gallatin Mountains. The open space sits on the south edge of the Gallatin Valley, due south of Bozeman off of 19th Street. The trail system begins in marshy meadows and climbs through aspen groves and Douglas fir to a ridge covered with juniper and sage. This hike follows a figure-8 pattern around Loops 1 and 3. At the top of Kirk Hill is a panoramic overlook with a map that identifies the peaks and canyons of the Madison Range.

Driving directions: From Main Street at the west end of Bozeman, drive south on 19th Avenue for 6 miles to the signed trailhead parking area on the left at a sharp right bend in the road. (En route, 19th Avenue becomes South 19th Road.) Turn left and park.

Hiking directions: Head south past the trailhead gate and cross the grassy meadow. Head up the foothills through the shady forest, crossing the footbridge over the irrigation ditch. Switchbacks lead uphill to a signed junction at 0.5 miles. The left fork leads to Loop 2 (Hike 33). Take the right fork uphill to junction F. Bear left on the cut-across trail, and traverse the hillside on the near-level path to junction D. Head uphill to the right through the pine and fir forest, reaching junction E at the top of the hill. Go to the right, following the hilltop ridge past Rocky Mountain juniper. On the left is a short side path to the panoramic overlook of the Madison Range. Back on the main trail, begin the descent back to the cut-across trail at junction F. Bear right and traverse the hillside again to junction D. This time, bear left and descend through the forest to junction C. Bear left again, completing the figure-8 at junction B. Take the right fork downhill, returning to the trailhead.

33. Kirk Hill (LOOP 2)

Hiking distance: 1.9 miles round trip
Hiking time: 1 hour
Elevation gain: 750 feet
Maps: U.S.G.S. Wheeler Mountain
      Kirk Hill Nature Trail Map

map
page 86

Summary of hike: Kirk Hill borders the Gallatin National Forest above Leverich Canyon and Hodgman Canyon. The open space has three interconnected self-guided loop trails. Interpretive signs identify the surrounding peaks, canyons, and the native and wild plants. From the ridge, a trail leaves the open space, connecting with Hyalite, Leverich, and Sourdough Canyons. This hike (Loop 2) is the largest and steepest of the three loops. The Kirk Hill trails are managed by the Museum of the Rockies and maintained by Kiwanis of the Bridgers.

Driving directions: Same as Hike 32.

Hiking directions: Hike past the trailhead gate and cross the meadow, heading south. Head up the foothills through the shady forest. Cross the wooden footbridge over the irrigation ditch, and zigzag up the trail, steadily gaining elevation. At 0.5 miles is a signed junction. Take the left fork, weaving up the trail to junction C. Bear left and begin the loop. Head east across the hillside through the forest of aspen, pine, and fir. The path curves south and heads steadily uphill, including some short, steep ascents. At the top, the trail levels out and crosses the hilltop. Stay to the right past junction G, which leads to Leverich Canyon, the Moser Jumpoff Road, and Bozeman Creek. Continue to junction E and Loop 1. Go to the right, returning downhill to the cut-across trail dividing Loops 1 and 3. Again stay to the right, completing the loop at junction C. Go left, back to junction B. Take the right fork downhill, returning to the trailhead.

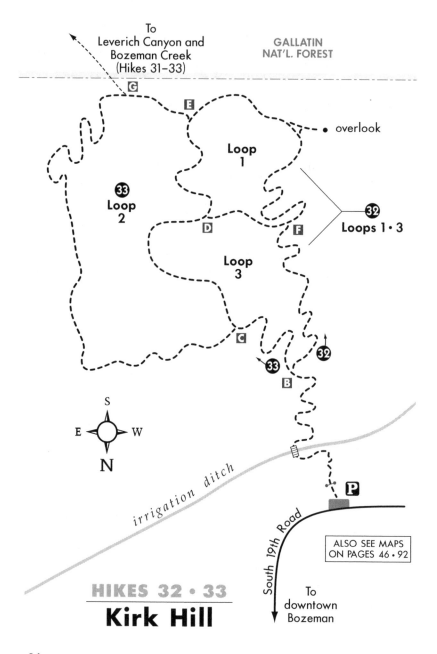

To
Leverich Canyon and
Bozeman Creek
(Hikes 31–33)

GALLATIN
NAT'L. FOREST

G

E

• overlook

Loop
1

33
Loop
2

D

F

32
Loops 1 • 3

Loop
3

C

33

B

32

S

E — W

N

irrigation ditch

South 19th Road

ALSO SEE MAPS
ON PAGES 46 • 92

P

To
downtown
Bozeman

HIKES 32 • 33
Kirk Hill

34. South Cottonwood Creek Trail

Hiking distance: 4.6 to 12 miles round trip
Hiking time: 2.5 to 6 hours
Elevation gain: 300 to 900 feet
Maps: U.S.G.S. Wheeler Mountain and Mount Blackmore
    Beartooth Publishing: Bozeman, Big Sky, W. Yellowstone

map
page 88

Summary of hike: South Cottonwood Creek flows from the upper reaches of Mount Blackmore to the Gallatin River at Gallatin Gateway. The creek gently tumbles down South Cottonwood Canyon, located on the north face of the Gallatin Range between Hyalite Canyon and Wheeler Mountain. The trail follows the creek on the northeast slope of Wheeler Mountain through a dense old-growth forest with lush riparian areas and meadows. The soft dirt path connects to Hyalite Canyon via the History Rock Trail at 6 miles (Hike 40) and the Mount Blackmore Trail at 8 miles.

Driving directions: From downtown Bozeman, drive 4 miles west on Main Street (Highway 191) toward Four Corners to Cottonwood Road at a stop light. Turn left and continue 7.6 miles to Cottonwood Canyon Road on the left. Turn left and drive 2.1 miles to the trailhead parking area at road's end.

From Big Sky, drive 27.7 miles north on Highway 191 to Cottonwood Road on the right. Turn right and continue 4.8 miles to Cottonwood Canyon Road on the right. Turn right and drive 2.1 miles to the trailhead parking area at road's end.

Hiking directions: Take the posted trail by the west corner of the parking area. Enter the lodgepole pine forest and zigzag up four switchbacks, gaining a quick 150 feet. Traverse the canyon wall along the mountain's contours. Gradually descend and pass through a trail gate to a meadow and South Cottonwood Creek. Veer left and cross a bridge over the creek. Climb the hill to a grassy meadow and follow the east slope upstream. Continue on the cliffside path high above the creek, skirting the northeast face of Wheeler Mountain. The trail alternates from shaded pockets of conifers to wildflower-covered meadows with scattered rock outcroppings. Cross a log bridge to the south bank of the creek at 1.3 miles, and cross again at 2 miles. Pass a trail on the left (which is difficult to see) that climbs to the Langhor Campground in Hyalite Canyon. For the next 2 miles, the path rises and falls from high above the creek to the streamside. The trail continues to a small Forest Service cabin by the History Rock Trail junction at 6 miles (Hike 40). The South Cottonwood Creek Trail continues south another 2 miles to Mount Blackmore. Choose your own turn-around spot.

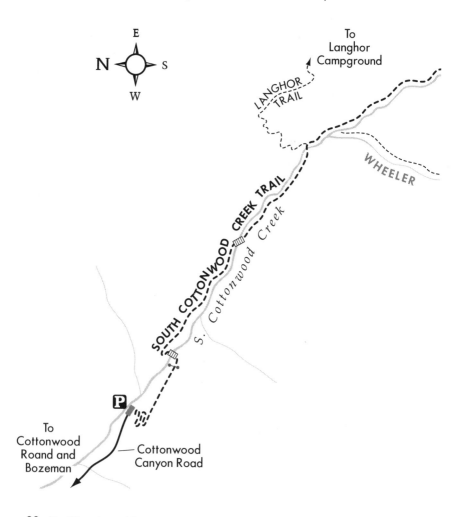

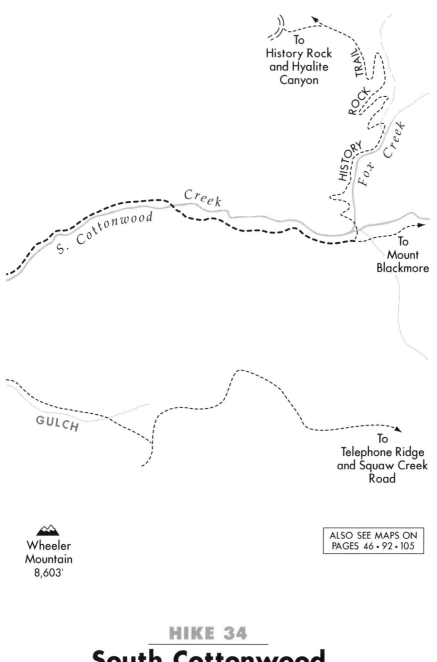

To
History Rock
and Hyalite
Canyon

ROCK TRAIL

HISTORY

Fox Creek

Creek

S. Cottonwood

To
Mount
Blackmore

GULCH

To
Telephone Ridge
and Squaw Creek
Road

Wheeler
Mountain
8,603'

ALSO SEE MAPS ON
PAGES 46 • 92 • 105

HIKE 34
South Cottonwood
Creek Trail

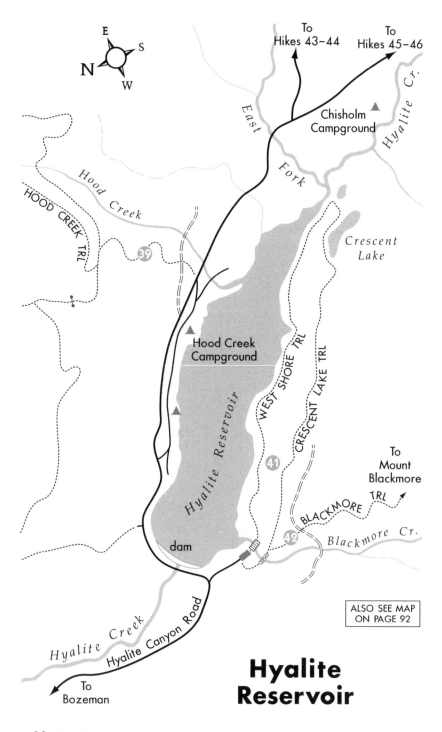

N E S W

To
Hikes 43-44

To
Hikes 45-46

East Fork

Hyalite Cr.

Chisholm
Campground

Hood Creek

HOOD CREEK TRL

39

Crescent
Lake

Hood Creek
Campground

WEST SHORE TRL

CRESCENT LAKE TRL

Hyalite Reservoir

41

To
Mount
Blackmore

BLACKMORE TRL

42

Blackmore Cr.

dam

ALSO SEE MAP
ON PAGE 92

Hyalite Creek

Hyalite Canyon Road

To
Bozeman

Hyalite
Reservoir

Hyalite Reservoir and Canyon

HIKES 35–46

map
next page

The Hyalite Canyon drainage is a 34,000-acre recreational oasis in the Gallatin Range just south of Bozeman. The centerpiece of the canyon is the Hyalite Reservoir, a 200-acre lake constructed in the late 1940s and enlarged in 1993. It serves as a water source for the city of Bozeman and the Gallatin Valley's agriculture. The picturesque reservoir sits in a broad, glacially sculpted U–shaped valley with canyons and steep-walled cirques. Framing the head of Hyalite Canyon are 10,000-foot mountain peaks. The reservoir is also a popular fishing area with cutthrout and arctic grayling.

A network of old logging roads, hiking, and biking trails lie within Hyalite Canyon. The trail system follows creeks, streams, and mountain slopes, leading to more than a dozen waterfalls, several alpine lakes, meadows covered in wild flowers, open ridges, and up to the surrounding peaks. Large boulders called erratics, deposited after the glacial ice melted, can be seen along the trails.

Hikes 35–37 begin near Langhor Campground, four miles downstream from the reservoir. Hike 37 explores the creekside, while Hikes 35 and 36 climb up the divide between Hyalite Canyon and Bozeman Creek (Hike 30.)

Hikes 38–42 are located around the perimeter of Hyalite Reservoir. The hikes range from an easy lakeside stroll to more strenuous hikes that climb through the surrounding canyons to views high above the reservoir.

Two major drainages feed the lake from the south—Hyalite Creek and the East Fork Hyalite Creek. Hike 43 is an easy hike on the East Fork to the picturesque Palisade Falls. Hike 45 continues up the drainage to the headwaters at Mount Chisholm.

The Hyalite Creek Trail—Hikes 45 and 46—is considered the most spectacular trail in the Bozeman area. Grotto Falls (Hike 45) is a short walk from the trailhead. Hike 46 continues 5.5 miles up the drainage, passing eleven waterfalls.

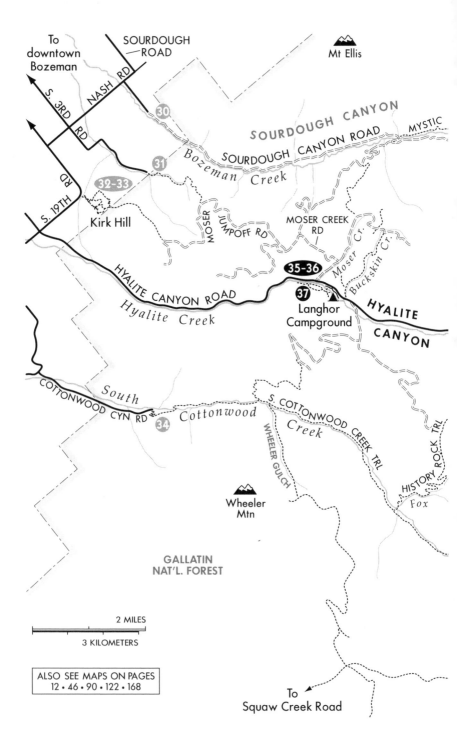

To
downtown
Bozeman

SOURDOUGH
ROAD

NASH RD

S. 3RD RD

S. 19TH RD

Mt Ellis

30

SOURDOUGH CANYON

SOURDOUGH CANYON ROAD

MYSTIC

Bozeman Creek

31

32-33

Kirk Hill

MOSER JUMPOFF RD

MOSER CREEK
RD

Moser Cr.

Buckskin Cr.

35-36

HYALITE CANYON ROAD

37

HYALITE

Langhor
Campground

CANYON

Hyalite Creek

COTTONWOOD CYN RD

South

34

Cottonwood

S. COTTONWOOD CREEK

Creek

WHEELER GULCH

S. COTTONWOOD CREEK TRL

HISTORY ROCK TRL

Fox

Wheeler
Mtn

GALLATIN
NAT'L. FOREST

2 MILES

3 KILOMETERS

ALSO SEE MAPS ON PAGES
12 • 46 • 90 • 122 • 168

To
Squaw Creek Road

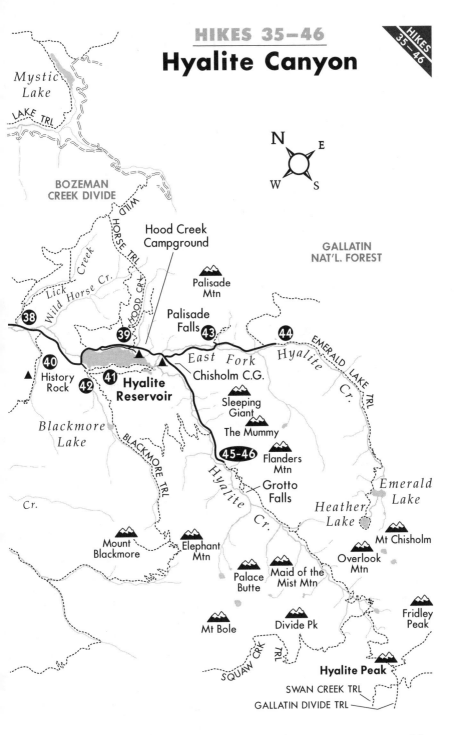

Hyalite Canyon

Mystic Lake

LAKE TRL

BOZEMAN CREEK DIVIDE

Hood Creek Campground

GALLATIN NAT'L. FOREST

WILD HORSE TRL

Lick Creek

Wild Horse Cr.

HOOD CRK

Palisade Mtn

Palisade Falls **43**

38

39

East Fork

44

EMERALD LAKE TRL

Hyalite Cr.

40

History Rock **42**

41 **Hyalite Reservoir**

Chisholm C.G.

Sleeping Giant

The Mummy

Blackmore Lake

BLACKMORE TRL

45-46

Flanders Mtn

Grotto Falls

Emerald Lake

Heather Lake

Cr.

Hyalite Cr.

Mount Blackmore

Elephant Mtn

Palace Butte

Maid of the Mist Mtn

Overlook Mtn

Mt Chisholm

Mt Bole

Divide Pk

Fridley Peak

SQUAW CRK TRL

Hyalite Peak

SWAN CREEK TRL

GALLATIN DIVIDE TRL

35. Moser Creek Loop

Hiking distance: 7.4 miles round trip
Hiking time: 3.5 hours
Elevation gain: 750 feet
Maps: U.S.G.S. Wheeler Mountain and Mount Ellis
      Beartooth Publishing: Bozeman, Big Sky, W. Yellowstone

map next page

Summary of hike: Moser Creek Road is an old logging road connecting Hyalite Canyon with Bozeman Creek and Sourdough Canyon Road. This loop hike begins alongside Moser Creek, just north of Langhor Campground, and climbs over the divide between the canyons into the Bozeman Creek drainage. The trail weaves through shady pine forests and grassy meadows covered in flowers. Throughout the hike are great vistas of the surrounding mountains and canyons.

Driving directions: From Main Street and 19th Avenue in Bozeman, drive south on 19th Avenue 7 miles to Hyalite Canyon Road on the left. (19th Avenue becomes South 19th Road at Kagy Boulevard.) Turn left and continue 5.6 miles to the unpaved road on the left, located a quarter mile north of Langhor Campground. Turn left and park in the pullout on the right. When the gate is open, drive 0.5 miles up the dirt road to a road fork. Curve left and park in the wide parking area on the left.

Hiking directions: From the lower gate at Hyalite Canyon Road, walk a half mile up unpaved Moser Creek Road to a road fork and the upper trailhead. Begin the loop to the left, hiking clockwise. Gently climb through lodgepole pines, pockets of aspen, and flower-covered grassy meadows, staying to the right at a road split. At 1.4 miles is a gated road on the right. The main road veers left to Leverich Canyon (Hike 31). Pass through the trail gate, and descend on the grass-covered two-track road. Pass an overlook of Mount Ellis to the south rim of Sourdough Canyon. Loop around a gulch and cross a feeder stream of Bozeman Creek at 2.8 miles. Follow the canyon contours to a horseshoe left bend at 4.4 miles. One hundred yards beyond the bend is an unmarked footpath on the right. The road descends to Bozeman

Creek—Hike 30. Instead, take the footpath on the right and head up the forested slope, passing through a bear lure station area. Skirt the south wall of the forested drainage. Steadily climb to the ridge, with vistas across Hyalite Canyon and the upper peaks. Descend past a trail gate to a large sloping meadow and a junction with a dirt road. Head downhill 0.9 miles to the right, completing the loop at the upper trailhead junction.

36. Moser—Buckskin Loop

Hiking distance: 4.7 mile loop
Hiking time: 2.5 hours
Elevation gain: 800 feet
Maps: U.S.G.S. Wheeler Mountain and Mount Ellis
　　　　　Beartooth Publishing: Bozeman, Big Sky, W. Yellowstone

*map
next page*

Summary of hike: Moser Creek and Buckskin Creek are tributaries of Hyalite Creek, draining down the east canyon wall. This hike parallels Moser Creek past its headwaters and returns along Buckskin Creek. The Moser-Buckskin Loop combines an old logging road with a forested footpath. The trails weave through flower-filled meadows and dense riparian forests.

Driving directions: Same as Hike 35.

Hiking directions: From the lower gate at Hyalite Canyon Road, walk a half mile up unpaved Moser Creek Road to a road fork and the upper trailhead. The left fork leads to Leverich Canyon. Begin the loop straight ahead on the right fork. Climb up the forested road to a huge sloping meadow at 1.4 miles. Continue on the road through the meadow, curving to the right. Steadily gain elevation and curve left on a horseshoe bend to a 4-way junction at 2.2 miles. Continue straight through and descend into the Buckskin Creek drainage. Climb a short distance to a left bend and an unsigned footpath on the right. Leave the road and take the path into the dense conifer forest. Follow the south side of the stream-fed canyon on the old, narrow roadbed with a view of Wheeler Mountain. Curve right and cross over trickling Buckskin Creek. Head down the north side of the creek, passing tree-rimmed meadows. A few paths on the left lead to the creek. At the lower end of a large meadow is a trail gate and junction. The left fork passes through the gate to Hyalite Canyon Road. Bear right and climb north through the meadow. Top the slope and enter a shaded forest, returning to Moser Creek Road and completing the loop. Return to the left.

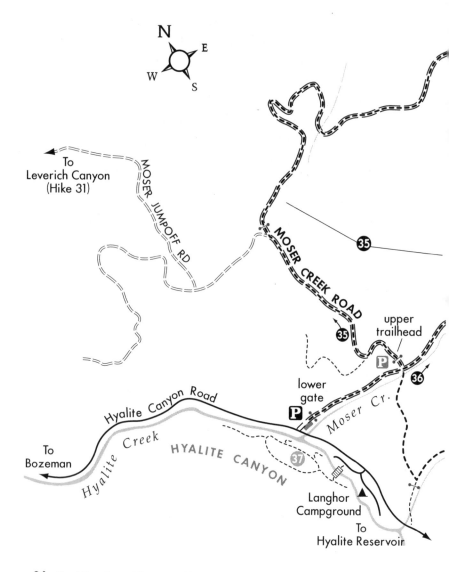

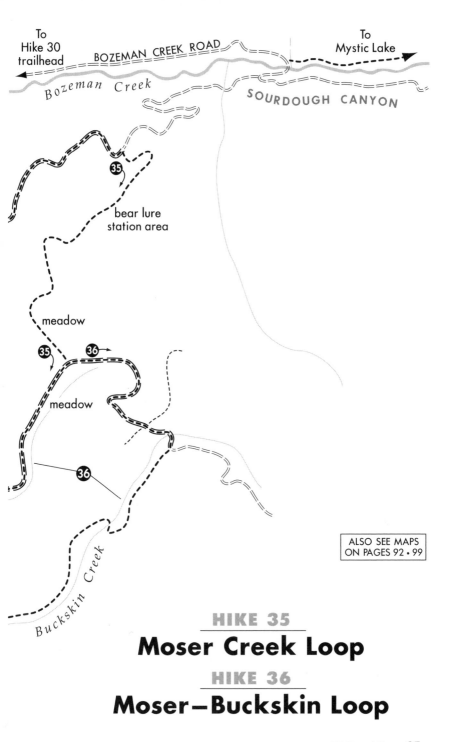

To
Hike 30
trailhead

BOZEMAN CREEK ROAD

To
Mystic Lake

Bozeman Creek

SOURDOUGH CANYON

35

bear lure
station area

meadow

35

36

meadow

36

ALSO SEE MAPS
ON PAGES 92 • 99

Buckskin Creek

HIKE 35
Moser Creek Loop
HIKE 36
Moser–Buckskin Loop

37. Langhor Loop Accessible Trail

Hiking distance: 0.3 mile loop to 2 miles round trip
Hiking time: 30 minutes to 1 hour
Elevation gain: Level
Maps: U.S.G.S. Wheeler Mountain
U.S.F.S. Hyalite Drainage map
Crystal Bench Maps: Bozeman, Montana

Summary of hike: The Langhor Loop Accessible Trail (also called the Hyalite Creek Interpretive Trail) is an easy forested stroll along the banks of Hyalite Creek. The wheelchair-accessible trail is at the north end of Langhor Campground, four miles downstream of Hyalite Reservoir. Throughout the scenic hike are wildflower-covered meadows, impressive rock formations, fishing accesses, and benches.

Driving directions: From Main Street and 19th Avenue in Bozeman, drive south on 19th Avenue (which becomes South 19th Road) 7 miles to Hyalite Canyon Road on the left. Turn left and continue 5.9 miles to the signed turnoff for Langhor Campground. Turn right and make an immediate right again to the signed trailhead parking area 0.1 mile ahead.

Hiking directions: Pass the trailhead sign and cross the wooden bridge over Hyalite Creek. A well-defined side path follows Hyalite Creek upstream and ends at a massive rock formation. A fork to the right climbs up the hillside and scrambles along the cliffs above the creek. Head back toward the bridge, and take the paved path to the north, following Hyalite Creek through a conifer forest. A short distance ahead is a trail fork, the beginning of the loop. Take the right fork downstream, staying close to the creek. Along the way, two paved side paths lead to the creek on the right. At the far end of the paved loop, a footpath continues north, following the creek through the forest. On the return portion of the paved loop, the trail continues through the forest past meadows with log benches. Complete the loop and return to the bridge.

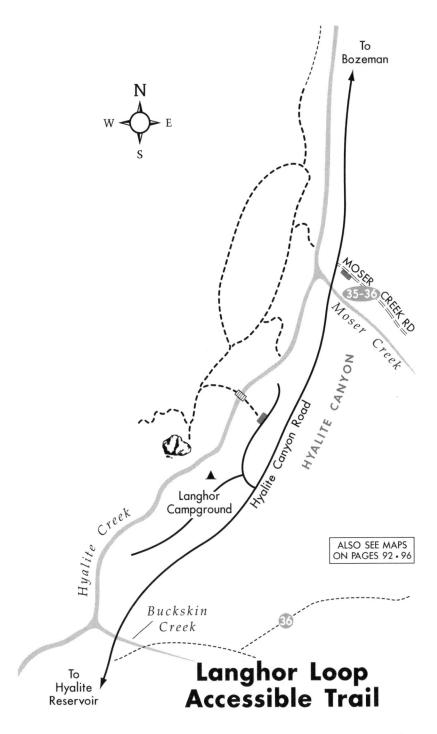

To
Bozeman

MOSER CREEK RD

35-36

Moser Creek

HYALITE CANYON

Hyalite Canyon Road

HYALITE CANYON

Hyalite Creek

▲

Langhor
Campground

ALSO SEE MAPS
ON PAGES 92 • 96

Buckskin
Creek

36

To
Hyalite
Reservoir

Langhor Loop
Accessible Trail

38. Lick Creek Loop to Bozeman Creek Divide

Hiking distance: 8 mile loop
Hiking time: 4 hours
Elevation gain: 1,150 feet
Maps: U.S.G.S. Mount Ellis
　　　　Beartooth Publishing: Bozeman, Big Sky, W. Yellowstone

map
next page

Summary of hike: Lick Creek, a tributary of Hyalite Creek, forms in the far northwest slope of Palisade Mountain. This hike follows Lick Creek Road, an abandoned logging road along the north side of the creek. The road continues past the creek's headwaters and meanders upward through a pristine forest to the Bozeman Creek Divide. Atop the divide are great views of the Hyalite peaks flanking the upper reaches of Hyalite Canyon. The trail connects with the Wild Horse Trail, which drops down to the South Fork of Bozeman Creek, and with the Hood Creek Trail that descends to Hyalite Reservoir (Hike 39).

Driving directions: From Main Street and 19th Avenue in Bozeman, drive south on 19th Avenue (which becomes South 19th Road) 7 miles to Hyalite Canyon Road on the left. Turn left and continue 8.4 miles to the unsigned dirt road on the left. It is located a half mile north of the History Rock Trail and 1.5 miles north of Hyalite Reservoir. Turn left and park in the small space on the left, staying clear of the gate.

For additional parking, large pullouts are on the creekside of Hyalite Canyon Road. They are located 0.2 miles on each side of the Lick Creek Road junction.

Hiking directions: Head up the unpaved road past the vehicle gate. Walk through open rolling meadows and pine forests. Pass through a cattle gate on the south edge of Lick Creek at 0.2 miles. At the top of the hill, just before a left bend in the road, is an old two-track roadbed on the right. Begin the loop, staying on the main road to the left. Steadily gain elevation, crossing several feeder streams. Pass a rocky road veering off to the left and stay straight, climbing the west wall of the gulch. Curve sharply to the left, then to the right, to open vistas across the entire Hyalite drainage, including Palisade Mountain, Sleeping Giant Mountain, Hyalite Peak, Elephant Mountain, and Mount Blackmore. Descend a quarter mile to the bottom of the hill and a faint trail on the right at 2.8 miles—the return loop. For now, continue straight ahead towards the divide. Near the summit, pass through an old logging area to a posted junction at the head of the Lick Creek drainage and the Bozeman Creek Divide. To the left, the Wild Horse Trail drops 1,300 feet over 1.5 miles to the South Fork of Bozeman Creek. Straight ahead, the Hood Creek Trail descends to Hyalite Reservoir (Hike 39). Retrace your steps to the return trail junction, now on the left. Take the side path through a grassy clearing and descend to Lick Creek. Cross the creek and merge with an old roadbed, curving to the right. Traverse the south wall of the drainage, completing the loop.

39. Hood Creek Trail to Wild Horse Creek

Hiking distance: 4.6 miles round trip
Hiking time: 2.5 hours
Elevation gain: 900 feet
Maps: U.S.G.S. Fridley Peak
                Beartooth Publishing: Bozeman, Big Sky, W. Yellowstone

map next page

Summary of hike: Hood Creek flows down the western slope of Palisade Mountain, feeding Hyalite Reservoir. Hood Creek Trail #436 (also known as the Wild Horse Trail) parallels Hood Creek, but the creek is never within sight or sound. The trail heads up the foothills of Palisade Mountain to great overlooks of the Hyalite Creek drainage, the East Fork of Hyalite Creek, Mount Blackmore, and Hyalite Reservoir. The trail connects to the Bozeman Creek drainage and Mystic Lake. It is also part of an 8.5-mile loop with Lick Creek Road (Hike 38).

Driving directions: From Main Street and 19th Avenue in Bozeman, drive south on 19th Avenue (which becomes South 19th Road) 7 miles to Hyalite Canyon Road on the left. Turn left and continue 11 miles, crossing to the east side of Hyalite Reservoir, to the signed Trail 436 on the left. It is located 20 yards south of the Hood Creek boat ramp and picnic area turnoff. Parking is not available at the trailhead, so turn right into the picnic area. Bear left at the first turn, and park in the day-use parking area by campsite 20.

Hiking directions: Hike back up the campground road to the signed trailhead on the east side of the main road. Head uphill to the northeast through the forest, and cross an old jeep road. Wide, sweeping switchbacks weave up the hill to an overlook of Hyalite Reservoir and Mount Blackmore. At one mile the trail reaches an old unpaved road. Follow the road 0.1 mile to the left and take the footpath to the right at the trail sign. Head uphill to an overlook of the East Fork and Main Fork of Hyalite Creek. Continue up the exposed northeast wall of the Hood Creek drainage, reaching the shade of the forest as the trail levels out. Cross a small bridge in a meadow over Wild Horse Creek at 2.3 miles, and head 50 yards to a junction. The right fork (straight ahead) leads to the Wild Horse Trail, Bozeman Creek, and Lick Creek (Hike 38). Go left on the old road and cross over Wild Horse Creek again. Slowly descend through meadows and evergreen pockets to a trail on the left with three large rocks and a blue cross-country ski diamond on a tree. (The Hood Creek Logging Road to the right, a gated fire road, leads one mile to an alternative access near the dam.) Bear left and traverse the hill, passing a trail gate. Complete the loop by the trail sign. Continue straight 0.1 miles and bear right, returning 1 mile downhill to the campground trailhead.

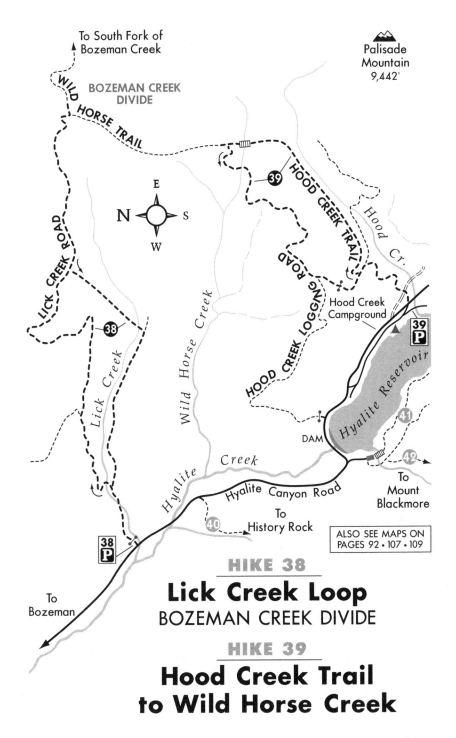

To South Fork of
Bozeman Creek

Palisade
Mountain
9,442'

BOZEMAN CREEK
DIVIDE

WILD HORSE TRAIL

HOOD CREEK TRAIL

Hood Cr.

N E S W

LICK CREEK ROAD

HOOD CREEK LOGGING ROAD

Hood Creek
Campground

39
P

Wild Horse Creek

38

Lick Creek

Hyalite Reservoir

DAM

41

Hyalite Creek

42

To
Mount
Blackmore

Hyalite Canyon Road

To
History Rock

40

ALSO SEE MAPS ON
PAGES 92 • 107 • 109

38
P

To
Bozeman

HIKE 38
Lick Creek Loop
BOZEMAN CREEK DIVIDE

HIKE 39
Hood Creek Trail
to Wild Horse Creek

40. History Rock Trail

Hiking distance: 2.4 miles round trip
Hiking time: 1 hour
Elevation gain: 300 feet
Maps: U.S.G.S. Fridley Peak
      U.S.F.S. Hyalite Drainage Map
      Crystal Bench Maps: Bozeman, Montana

Summary of hike: History Rock is a sandstone rock outcropping with natural and cultural history. Signatures and inscriptions by early settlers and hunters, dating back to the mid-1800s, are carved into the distinct outcropping. Current inscriptions are also present. The History Rock Trail begins a mile downstream of Hyalite Reservoir and gradually climbs through meadows and lodgepole pines, paralleling History Rock Creek to the natural rock monument. Beyond History Rock, the trail climbs to the divide and descends for several miles, linking the Hyalite drainage with South Cottonwood Creek. This trail can be hiked as a one-way, 11-mile shuttle, leaving a shuttle car at the South Cottonwood Creek Trailhead (Hike 34).

Driving directions: From Main Street and 19th Avenue in Bozeman, drive south on 19th Avenue (which becomes South 19th Road) 7 miles to Hyalite Canyon Road on the left. Turn left and continue 8.8 miles to the History Rock turnoff on the right, one mile before Hyalite Reservoir. Turn right and park 100 feet ahead in the trailhead parking area.

Hiking directions: From the parking area, follow the log-bordered trail southwest through the meadow. Beyond the meadow, enter a forest and begin ascending the mountain slope. At 1.2 miles, the distinct and etched History Rock appears on the right. After studying the outcrop, return along the same path for a 2.4-mile round trip hike.

To extend the hike, climb two miles (gaining 1,000 feet) to the divide above South Cottonwood Creek. Descend two more miles to South Cottonwood Creek—Hike 34. For the shuttle hike, reference the map for Hike 34.

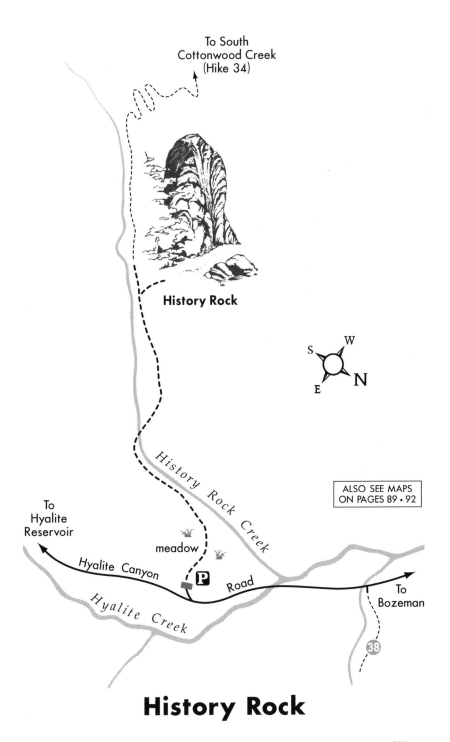

To South
Cottonwood Creek
(Hike 34)

History Rock

S W
E N

ALSO SEE MAPS
ON PAGES 89 · 92

History Rock Creek

To
Hyalite
Reservoir

meadow

Hyalite Canyon

P

Road

Hyalite Creek

To
Bozeman

38

History Rock

41. Crescent Lake
CRESCENT LAKE—WEST SHORE LOOP

Hiking distance: 2.5 mile loop
Hiking time: 1.5 hours
Elevation gain: 240 feet
Maps: U.S.G.S. Fridley Peak
U.S.F.S. Hyalite Drainage Map
Crystal Bench Maps: Bozeman, Montana

Summary of hike: Crescent Lake is a small crescent-shaped tarn surrounded by picturesque mountains on the southwest corner of Hyalite Reservoir. The Crescent Lake Trail meanders through the forest on an easy grade to the lake. The return route on the West Shore Trail loops back along the entire western shoreline of Hyalite Reservoir.

Driving directions: From Main Street and 19th Avenue in Bozeman, drive south on 19th Avenue (which becomes South 19th Road) 7 miles to Hyalite Canyon Road on the left. Turn left and continue 9.9 miles to the trailhead parking area on the right. Hyalite Reservoir is to the left.

Hiking directions: The hike begins on the Blackmore Trail at the north end of the parking area. Take the trail to a log crossing over Blackmore Creek, an inlet stream of Hyalite Reservoir. Across the creek is a signed junction. The right fork continues on to Blackmore Lake—Hike 42. Take the left fork on the Crescent Lake Trail. Continue one mile through the forest to the north shore of Crescent Lake. The trail follows the northeast shore of the lake before heading to a pond at the southern tip of the reservoir. Head to the left on the West Shore Trail. The trail returns along the reservoir's west shore. Near the trailhead, cross over Blackmore Creek on a wooden bridge, completing the loop.

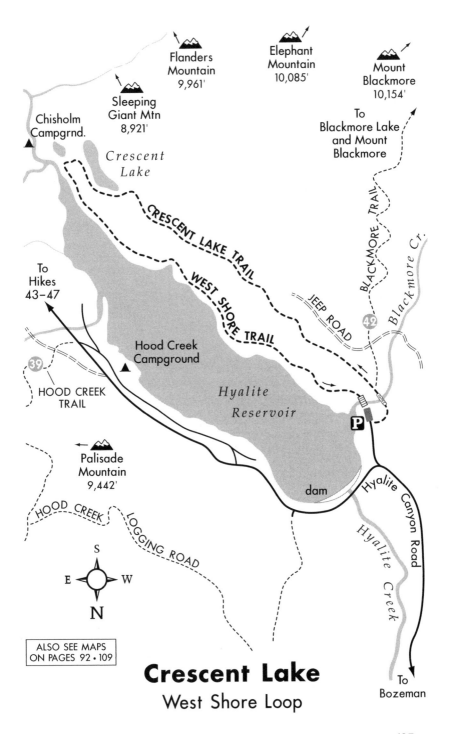

Flanders
Mountain
9,961'

Elephant
Mountain
10,085'

Mount
Blackmore
10,154'

Sleeping
Giant Mtn
8,921'

Chisholm
Campgrnd.

*Crescent
Lake*

To
Blackmore Lake
and Mount
Blackmore

CRESCENT LAKE TRAIL

WEST SHORE TRAIL

BLACKMORE TRAIL

Blackmore Cr.

JEEP ROAD

42

To
Hikes
43–47

Hood Creek
Campground

39

HOOD CREEK
TRAIL

*Hyalite
Reservoir*

P

Palisade
Mountain
9,442'

dam

Hyalite Canyon Road

Hyalite Creek

HOOD CREEK

LOGGING ROAD

S

E W

N

ALSO SEE MAPS
ON PAGES 92 • 109

Crescent Lake
West Shore Loop

To
Bozeman

42. Blackmore Trail to Blackmore Lake

Hiking distance: 3.3 miles round trip
Hiking time: 2 hours
Elevation gain: 500 feet
Maps: U.S.G.S. Fridley Peak
U.S.F.S. Hyalite Drainage Map
Crystal Bench Maps: Bozeman, Montana

Summary of hike: Blackmore Lake sits on the northern slope of Mount Blackmore at 7,300 feet, 600 feet above the west shore of Hyalite Reservoir. A dense pine forest and meadow surround the lake beneath Mount Blackmore and Elephant Mountain. The 5-mile-long Blackmore Trail begins at the west shore of Hyalite Reservoir and leads to Blackmore Lake en route to the top of Mount Blackmore, high above the South Cottonwood Creek and Hyalite Creek drainages.

Driving directions: From Main Street and 19th Avenue in Bozeman, drive south on 19th Avenue (which becomes South 19th Road) 7 miles to Hyalite Canyon Road on the left. Turn left and continue 9.9 miles to the trailhead parking area on the right. Hyalite Reservoir is to the left.

Hiking directions: Take the signed Blackmore Trail to a log crossing over Blackmore Creek and a trail junction. The left fork leads to Crescent Lake—Hike 41. Stay on the Blackmore Trail to the right. At 0.4 miles, cross an old jeep road and zigzag uphill through the forest. As you near the lake, which is not within view, there is a short but steep descent that leads to the southeast corner of Blackmore Lake. The main trail continues along the east side of the lake into a meadow where Blackmore Creek flows placidly. This is the turn-around spot. Return along the same trail.

To hike farther, the trail continues 3.5 miles and gains 2,800 feet to Mount Blackmore, then descends to South Cottonwood Creek.

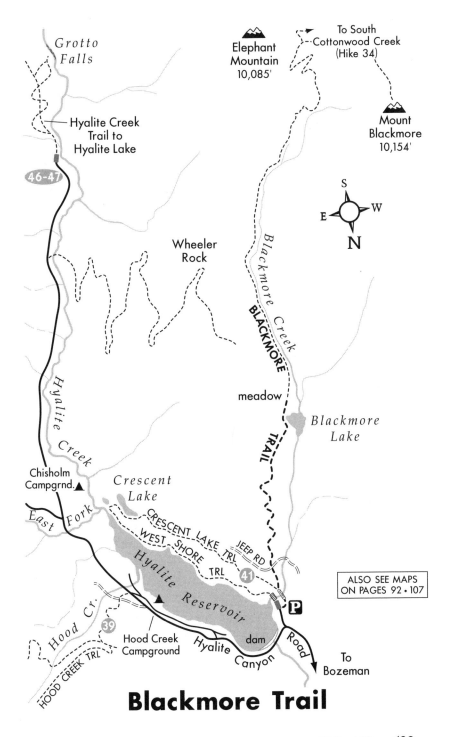

Grotto
Falls

Elephant
Mountain
10,085'

To South
Cottonwood Creek
(Hike 34)

Hyalite Creek
Trail to
Hyalite Lake

Mount
Blackmore
10,154'

46-47

S

E — W

N

Wheeler
Rock

Blackmore Creek

BLACKMORE

TRAIL

meadow

Blackmore
Lake

Hyalite Creek

Chisholm
Campgrnd. ▲

Crescent
Lake

East Fork

CRESCENT LAKE TRL

WEST SHORE

TRL

JEEP RD

41

ALSO SEE MAPS
ON PAGES 92 • 107

Hyalite Reservoir

▲

Hood Cr.

39

Hood Creek
Campground

Hyalite Canyon

dam

Road

To
Bozeman

HOOD CREEK TRL

Blackmore Trail

43. Palisade Falls
EAST FORK of HYALITE CREEK

Hiking distance: 1.2 miles round trip
Hiking time: 30 minutes
Elevation gain: 250 feet
Maps: U.S.G.S. Fridley Peak
         Beartooth Publishing: Bozeman, Big Sky, W. Yellowstone

map
page 112

Summary of hike: Palisade Falls is a towering cataract that drops more than 80 feet off a vertical rock wall at the southern base of Palisade Mountain. The water pours from a notch in the scalloped columnar basalt, the result of an ancient lava flow. From the tree-lined ridge, the waterfall fans out in a mosaic of white cascades tumbling down the rocks. The forested trail is an easy, paved, wheelchair-accessible path that sits 700 feet above the Hyalite Reservoir. The hike begins at the East Fork of Hyalite Creek and leads 0.6 miles to a bridge fronting the falls. There are picnic sites at the trailhead.

Driving directions: From Main Street and 19th Avenue in Bozeman, drive south on 19th Avenue (which becomes South 19th Road) 7 miles to Hyalite Canyon Road on the left. Turn left and continue 11.7 miles, crossing to the east side of Hyalite Reservoir, to a road fork. Take the left fork one mile to the Palisade Falls parking and picnic area on the left.

Hiking directions: Take the paved path past the posted trailhead, and weave through the forest on a gentle uphill grade. The jagged ridgeline of Palisade Mountain can be seen through the pine and fir trees. Pass a talus slope on the left at the first view of the falls. Cross a wooden bridge over the creek to the end of the trail at the base of Palisade Falls. Side paths to the right climb up the slippery hillside on loose gravel to additional views. Use caution and good judgement if you venture beyond the bridge.

44. Emerald Lake Trail

Hiking distance: 10 miles round trip
Hiking time: 5 hours
Elevation gain: 2,000 feet

map
page 113

Maps: U.S.G.S. Fridley Peak
U.S.F.S. Hyalite Drainage map
Beartooth Publishing: Bozeman, Big Sky, W. Yellowstone

Summary of hike: The Emerald Lake Trail (also called East Fork Hyalite Creek Trail) leads 5 miles up the creek to the head of the canyon, where Emerald Lake and Heather Lake sit in a mountainous alpine meadow. The towering rock walls of Mount Chisholm and Overlook Mountain drop sharply to the shore, forming a dramatic cirque around the lakes. The trail passes Horsetail Falls, a long, narrow waterfall tumbling off the west canyon wall, and another 60-foot waterfall farther up the creek drainage.

Driving directions: Follow the directions for Hike 43, then continue another 1.1 miles past the Palisade Falls parking area to the trailhead parking at the end of the road.

Hiking directions: The trail heads south through the forest above the East Fork of Hyalite Creek, paralleling the creek to its headwaters. Head up the drainage and cross a log bridge at 0.5 miles. Horsetail Falls, a series of tall, narrow braids of water, can be seen on the west canyon wall at 1.5 miles. At 3 miles, the trail reaches the banks of the creek in a small meadow. Across the canyon are Flanders Mountain and The Mummy. Ascend the hill, zigzagging up 10 switchbacks and gaining 400 feet in a half mile. At the edge of the cliff by the second switchback is the beautiful 60-foot waterfall. At the top of the switchbacks are great views back down the canyon. The trail levels out near the base of Mount Chisholm. Cross a log bridge over the East Fork Hyalite Creek, and head through the high open meadow with stands of conifers. Four switchbacks lead to an array of wildflowers in a second meadow. Cross a culvert over a stream to an overlook of the lake and a trail split. The left fork follows the northeast

shoreline and circles the lake. The right fork—the main trail—
continues past the north end of Emerald Lake, reaching Heather
Lake a half mile farther. The trail circles Heather Lake in a cirque
at the base of 10,000-foot peaks. Return along the same route.

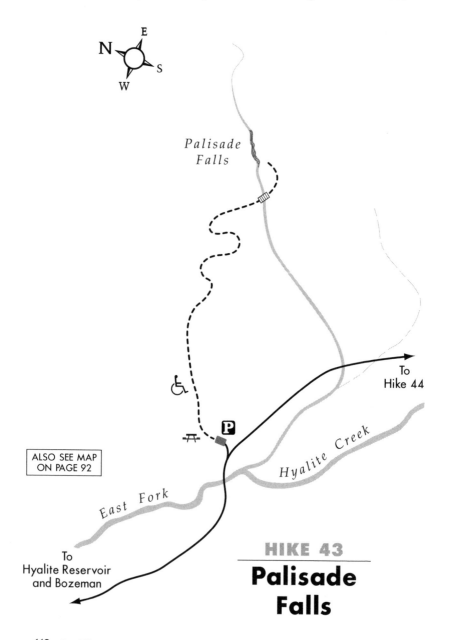

Palisade
Falls

To
Hike 44

ALSO SEE MAP
ON PAGE 92

Hyalite Creek

East Fork

To
Hyalite Reservoir
and Bozeman

HIKE 43
Palisade
Falls

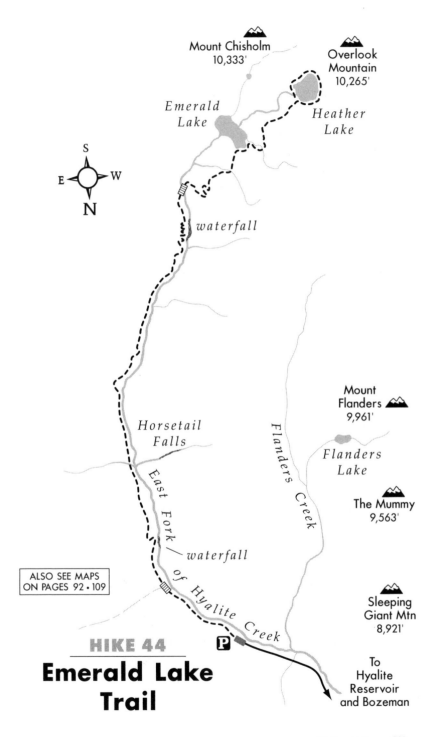

Mount Chisholm
10,333'

Overlook
Mountain
10,265'

*Emerald
Lake*

*Heather
Lake*

S

E ⊕ W

N

waterfall

Mount
Flanders
9,961'

*Horsetail
Falls*

*Flanders
Lake*

Flanders Creek

The Mummy
9,563'

East Fork

waterfall

ALSO SEE MAPS
ON PAGES 92 • 109

of Hyalite Creek

Sleeping
Giant Mtn
8,921'

P

HIKE 44
**Emerald Lake
Trail**

To
Hyalite
Reservoir
and Bozeman

45. Grotto Falls

HYALITE CREEK

Hiking distance: 2.5 miles round trip
Hiking time: 1.25 hours
Elevation gain: 250 feet
Maps: U.S.G.S. Fridley Peak
   U.S.F.S. Hyalite Drainage map
   Beartooth Publishing: Bozeman, Big Sky, W. Yellowstone

map
page 116

Summary of hike: Grotto Falls is a wide and magnificent waterfall on Hyalite Creek. The cataract is in the forested canyon above Hyalite Reservoir, beneath towering Flanders Mountain and Elephant Mountain. The shady 1.25-mile trail has a gradual grade and is wheelchair accessible. Along the gravel path are log benches that are placed at scenic vista points overlooking Hyalite Creek. This hike is the first section of the Hyalite Creek Trail (Hike 46), which passes ten additional waterfalls en route to Hyalite Lake.

Driving directions: From Main Street and 19th Avenue in Bozeman, drive south on 19th Avenue (which becomes South 19th Road) 7 miles to Hyalite Canyon Road on the left. Turn left and continue 11.7 miles, crossing to the east side of Hyalite Reservoir, to a road fork. Take the right fork 1.9 miles to the Hyalite Creek/Grotto Falls parking area at the end of the road.

Hiking directions: Hike south past the trailhead sign along the wide trail. A short distance ahead is a junction with the Hyalite Creek Trail. These two trails crisscross each other four times en route to the falls. Each junction is well marked. The Grotto Falls Trail is the wider trail which leads to the waterfall, where a log bench overlooks the beautiful falls.

To extend the hike, continue with Hike 46. The scenic path leads another 4 miles (gaining 1,800 feet) to Hyalite Lake and the Hyalite Basin. En route, the trail passes ten stair-stepping waterfalls.

46. Hyalite Creek Trail to Hyalite Lake

Hiking distance: 11 miles round trip

Hiking time: 5 hours

map
page 117

Elevation gain: 1,900 feet

Maps: U.S.G.S. Fridley Peak, U.S.F.S. Hyalite Drainage map
  Beartooth Publishing: Bozeman, Big Sky, W. Yellowstone

Summary of hike: The Hyalite Creek Trail is considered the most spectacular hike in the Bozeman area. The trail passes eleven waterfalls in a deep canyon with massive cliff walls and majestic peaks. The hike ends at Hyalite Lake, a high alpine lake in a horseshoe-shaped basin (front cover photo). The lake is surrounded by the craggy pinnacles of Fridley Peak and Hyalite Peak.

Driving directions: Same as Hike 45.

Hiking directions: The Hyalite Creek Trail heads south on a wide path through the forest, paralleling the creek to its headwaters. The Grotto Falls Trail (Hike 45) begins on the same path but zigzags through the forest, crossing the Hyalite Creek Trail four times. At the last junction, the left fork bypasses Grotto Falls and heads up the canyon. Twin Falls is on the west canyon wall to the south of Elephant Mountain, two adjacent waterfalls plunging off the sheer cliffs. At 1.4 miles, a signed side path leads to Arch Falls on the right, a falls with a natural rock arch. At 2.2 miles, a signed detour to the left leads to Silken Skein Falls. A short distance ahead on the right is an unnamed 20-foot waterfall in a rock bowl with a pool. At 3 miles, a short detour leads to Champagne Falls, an 80-foot waterfall in a narrow fern-lined rock grotto. At 3.7 miles are three successive waterfalls—Chasm, Shower, and Apex Falls. Cross a log footbridge over Hyalite Creek below the base of Apex Falls. Rock hop over Shower Creek, then loop back and recross the creek at a stunning cascade. Cross back to the east side of Hyalite Creek and pass S'il Vous Plait Falls. Recross the creek at the base of Alpine Falls and traverse the cliff overlooking the entire U-shaped canyon. A short distance ahead is a signed junction at 5.3 miles. Bear left to a second junction. The right fork leads to Hyalite Peak, 2 miles ahead. The left fork leads 100 yards to an overlook of Hyalite Lake at the base of Fridley Peak and Hyalite Peak. Descend to the shoreline in the dramatic mountain bowl. Return on the same trail.

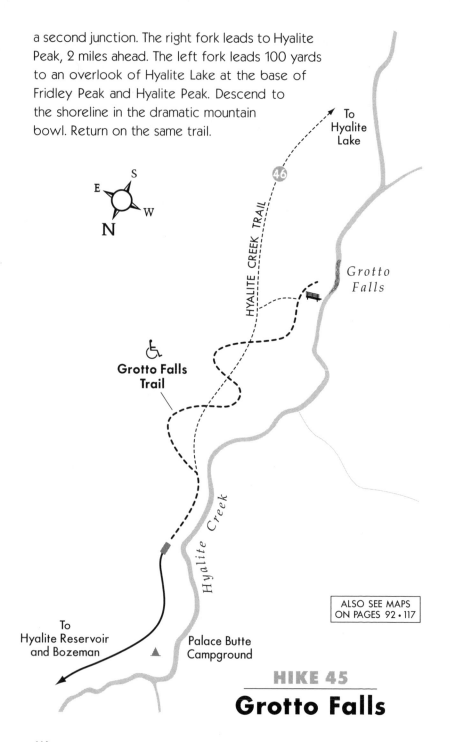

To
Hyalite
Lake

46

HYALITE CREEK TRAIL

*Grotto
Falls*

**Grotto Falls
Trail**

Hyalite Creek

ALSO SEE MAPS
ON PAGES 92 • 117

To
Hyalite Reservoir
and Bozeman

Palace Butte
Campground

HIKE 45

Grotto Falls

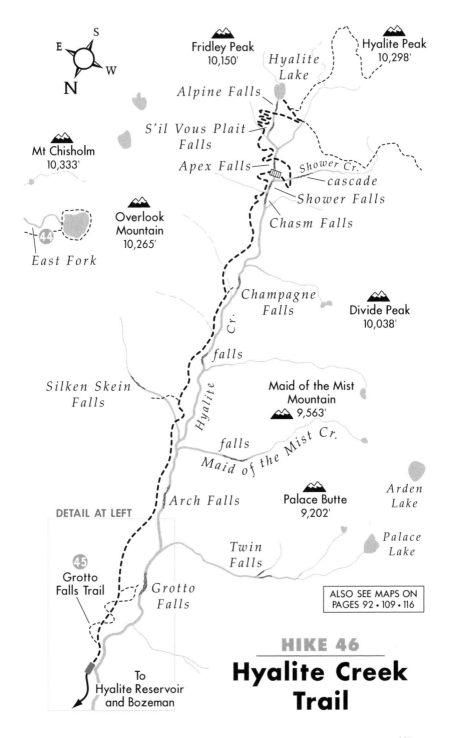

E · S
N · W

Fridley Peak
10,150'

Hyalite Peak
10,298'

Hyalite
Lake

Alpine Falls

S'il Vous Plait
Falls

Mt Chisholm
10,333'

Apex Falls

Shower Cr.

cascade

Shower Falls

Chasm Falls

Overlook
Mountain
10,265'

44

East Fork

Champagne
Falls

Divide Peak
10,038'

falls

Cr.

Silken Skein
Falls

Hyalite

Maid of the Mist
Mountain
9,563'

falls

Maid of the Mist Cr.

Arch Falls

Palace Butte
9,202'

Arden
Lake

Palace
Lake

DETAIL AT LEFT

Twin
Falls

45

Grotto
Falls Trail

Grotto
Falls

ALSO SEE MAPS ON
PAGES 92 · 109 · 116

ALSO SEE MAPS ON
PAGES 92 · 109 · 116

To
Hyalite Reservoir
and Bozeman

HIKE 46
Hyalite Creek Trail

47. Bear Trap Canyon Trail

Hiking distance: 0.5 to 14 miles round trip
Hiking time: 30 minutes to all day
Elevation gain: 50 feet to 500 feet
Maps: U.S.G.S. Bear Trap Creek, Norris, Ennis Lake
U.S.F.S. Gallatin National Forest: West Half
BLM Bear Trap Canyon Wilderness Guide

Summary of hike: Bear Trap Canyon is a spectacular drainage encompassing 6,000 acres in the Lee Metcalf Wilderness within the Madison Range. The Madison River, its headwaters in Yellowstone, rages through the remote, roadless canyon for 9 miles, from Ennis Lake to the Madison River Bridge. It is a well known and popular fishing area between Bozeman and Norris. The trail hugs the east shore of the river, winding along sheer rock cliffs carved 1,500 feet deep by the river. The only hiking access is from the north, so solitude increases deeper into the canyon. The full length of the trail is seven miles. At the southern end is the powerhouse and dam holding back Ennis Lake. Hiking is prohibited around the dam.

Bear Trap Canyon has rattlesnakes. As a precaution, a snakebite kit is recommended.

Driving directions: From Bozeman, drive 9 miles west to Four Corners on Highway 191. Continue 20.7 miles west on Highway 84 to Bear Trap Road on the left. It is located by the Bear Trap Recreational Area sign, just before the bridge crossing the Madison River. Turn left and drive on the gravel road 3.2 miles along the east side of the river. The trailhead parking area is at the end of the road.

Hiking directions: From the parking area, hike south along the east bank of the Madison River. The wide trail soon becomes a footpath and follows the eastern edge of the cliffs. The coarse canyon continually becomes steeper and deeper, reaching the mouth of Bear Trap Creek at 3.5 miles. It is a level area with campsites and a good spot to take a break. The Madison Powerhouse is at 9 miles. Hike as deep into the rocky canyon as you choose, returning on the same path.

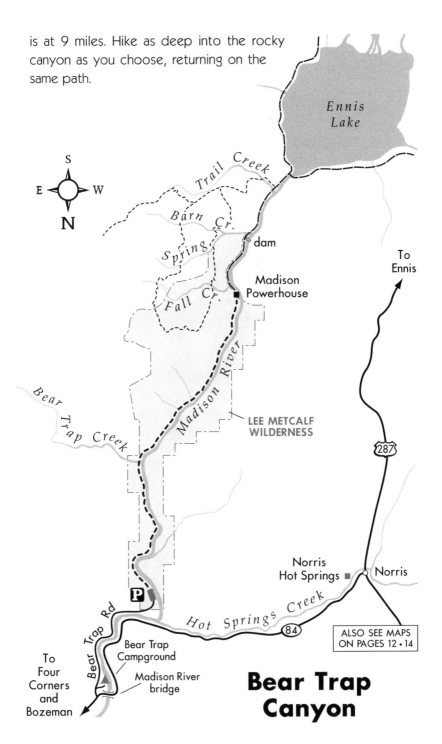

Ennis
Lake

Trail Creek

Barn Cr.

Spring

dam

Madison
Powerhouse

To
Ennis

Fall Cr.

Madison River

LEE METCALF
WILDERNESS

Bear Trap Creek

287

Norris
Hot Springs ■ ○ Norris

P

Bear Trap Rd

Hot Springs Creek

84

ALSO SEE MAPS
ON PAGES 12 • 14

To
Four
Corners
and
Bozeman

Bear Trap
Campground

Madison River
bridge

Bear Trap
Canyon

S

E W

N

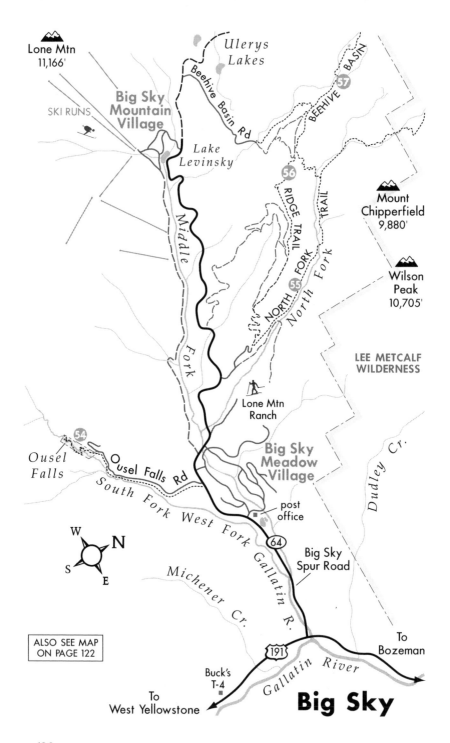

Lone Mtn
11,166'

*Ulerys
Lakes*

Big Sky
Mountain
Village

SKI RUNS

Beehive Basin Rd

BEEHIVE BASIN

37

*Lake
Levinsky*

56

RIDGE TRAIL

NORTH FORK TRAIL

*Middle
Fork*

NORTH FORK

North Fork

55

Mount
Chipperfield
9,880'

Wilson
Peak
10,705'

LEE METCALF
WILDERNESS

Lone Mtn
Ranch

54

Big Sky
Meadow
Village

*Ousel
Falls*

O*usel Falls Rd*

South Fork West Fork Gallatin R.

post
office

64

Big Sky
Spur Road

Dudley Cr.

W   N
S   E

Michener Cr.

Gallatin R.

ALSO SEE MAP
ON PAGE 122

191

To
Bozeman

Buck's
T-4

To
West Yellowstone

Gallatin River

Big Sky

Gallatin Canyon

HIKES 48—58

map
next page

The Gallatin Canyon is a narrow cleft that lies between the Gallatin Range and the Madison Range 14 miles southwest of Bozeman. The tumbling whitewater of the Gallatin River cascades through the serpentine gorge, splitting the mountain ranges. The river ultimately flows into the south end of the Gallatin Valley. US Highway 191 snakes alongside the Gallatin River, connecting Bozeman with Big Sky and West Yellowstone.

The Gallatin Range to the east of the canyon divides Gallatin Canyon from Paradise Valley. The 10,000-foot mountain range stretches from Bozeman to Yellowstone National Park. The diverse area has wide valleys; open meadows; numerous creeks; and the 26,000-acre Gallatin Petrified Forest, an ancient rock forest with preserved tropical trees. Hikes 51, 53, and 58 are creekside paths along canyons that emerge from the Gallatins. Hike 50 is a level trail that hugs the cliffs parallel to the Gallatin River.

The dramatic Madison Range to the west divides the Gallatin Canyon from Madison Valley. The range includes the 256,000-acre Lee Metcalf Wilderness and the landmark Spanish Peaks, a cluster of jagged, snow-capped peaks visible from Bozeman. The 60-mile Madison Range has 10,000- and 11,000-foot peaks. It is the second highest range in Montana, following the 12,000-foot Beartooth Mountains. The Madison Range is home to U-shaped glacial valleys, subalpine meadows, serrated ridges, thick forests, nearly 200 lakes, and a mosaic of trails that connect canyon drainages on both sides of the range.

The Spanish Peaks are accessed on the north from Hikes 48 and 49. The Cascade Creek Trail—Hike 52—is one of the most popular trails in the area. Hikes 55—57 head into the Spanish Peaks from the south near Big Sky. Ousel Falls—Hike 54—is a beautiful waterfall just south of Big Sky.

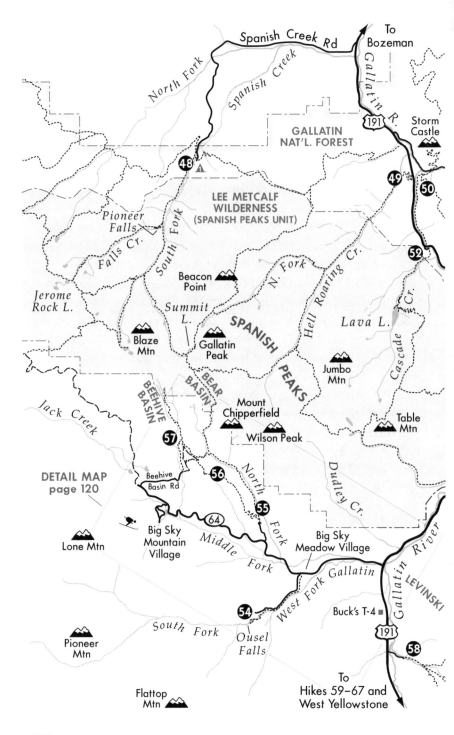

To
Bozeman

Spanish Creek Rd

North Fork

Spanish Creek

Gallatin R.

GALLATIN
NAT'L. FOREST

191

Storm
Castle

48

49

50

LEE METCALF
WILDERNESS
(SPANISH PEAKS UNIT)

Pioneer
Falls

Falls Cr.

South Fork

N. Fork

Hell Roaring Cr.

52

Cascade Cr.

Beacon
Point

Lava L.

Jerome
Rock L.

Summit
L.

SPANISH

Blaze
Mtn

Gallatin
Peak

Jumbo
Mtn

PEAKS

Table
Mtn

Jack Creek

BEEHIVE
BASIN

BEAR
BASIN

Mount
Chipperfield

Wilson Peak

Dudley Cr.

DETAIL MAP
page 120

57

Beehive
Basin Rd

56

North Fork

55

Lone Mtn

Big Sky
Mountain
Village

64

Middle Fork

Big Sky
Meadow Village

Gallatin River

LEVINSKI

West Fork Gallatin

Buck's T-4

191

54

Pioneer
Mtn

South Fork

Ousel
Falls

58

Flattop
Mtn

To
Hikes 59–67 and
West Yellowstone

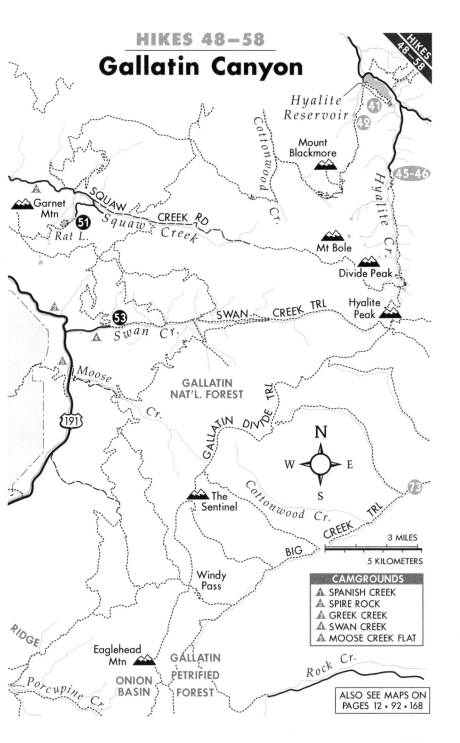

Gallatin Canyon

*Hyalite
Reservoir*

41

42

Cottonwood Cr.

Mount
Blackmore

45-46

Hyalite Cr.

Garnet
Mtn

SQUAW

51

Squaw Creek

CREEK RD

Rat L.

Mt Bole

Divide Peak

SWAN CREEK TRL

53

Swan Cr.

Hyalite
Peak

Moose

GALLATIN
NAT'L. FOREST

GALLATIN DIVIDE TRL

191

Cr.

The
Sentinel

Cottonwood Cr.

N

W ⬥ E

S

73

CREEK TRL

BIG

3 MILES

5 KILOMETERS

Windy
Pass

CAMGROUNDS
⛺ SPANISH CREEK
⛺ SPIRE ROCK
⛺ GREEK CREEK
⛺ SWAN CREEK
⛺ MOOSE CREEK FLAT

RIDGE

Eaglehead
Mtn

GALLATIN

ONION
BASIN

PETRIFIED

Porcupine Cr.

FOREST

Rock Cr.

ALSO SEE MAPS ON
PAGES 12 • 92 • 168

48. Pioneer Falls
SOUTH FORK of SPANISH CREEK

Hiking distance: 7.5 miles round trip
Hiking time: 3.5 hours
Elevation gain: 800 feet
Maps: U.S.G.S. Beacon Point and Willow Swamp
      Rocky Mountain Surveys: Spanish Peaks

Summary of hike: Pioneer Falls is a full-bodied 40-foot cascade on Falls Creek, a tributary of the South Fork of Spanish Creek. The trail heads into the Lee Metcalf Wilderness, part of the Spanish Peaks Unit of the Madison Range. The near-level trail parallels the South Fork of Spanish Creek (back cover photo) beneath Gallatin Peak, Beacon Point, and Blaze Mountain. Several short, steep switchbacks ascend up the canyon along Falls Creek to Pioneer Falls. The Spanish Creek Road to the trailhead is a public access road through Ted Turner's Flying D Ranch. It is a scenic drive with great vistas along the North Fork of Spanish Creek.

Driving directions: From Four Corners 9 miles west of Bozeman, take Highway 191 south towards the Gallatin Canyon. Drive 13.1 miles to Spanish Creek Road on the right. Turn right and continue on Spanish Creek Road 9 miles to the Spanish Creek Campground and trailhead parking area.

From Big Sky, Spanish Creek Road is 20.7 miles north on Highway 191.

Hiking directions: Take the trail to the west, crossing the bridge over the South Fork of Spanish Creek. Bear left and head upstream through lodgepole pines and Engelmann spruce on the South Fork Trail. At a half mile, enter the Lee Metcalf Wilderness, and cross several streams while staying close to the South Fork. At 3 miles is a posted junction with the Falls Creek Trail. Take the right fork along Falls Creek. Switchbacks continue for .75 miles, rising 450 feet to the brink of Pioneer Falls. Shortly before reaching the top, a side trail leads to a magnificent view of the waterfall. Return on the same trail.

To extend the hike, the Falls Creek Trail continues to Jerome Rock Lakes, just below the Madison Divide. The South Fork Trail continues south to Mirror Lake, Summit Lake, and Big Sky.

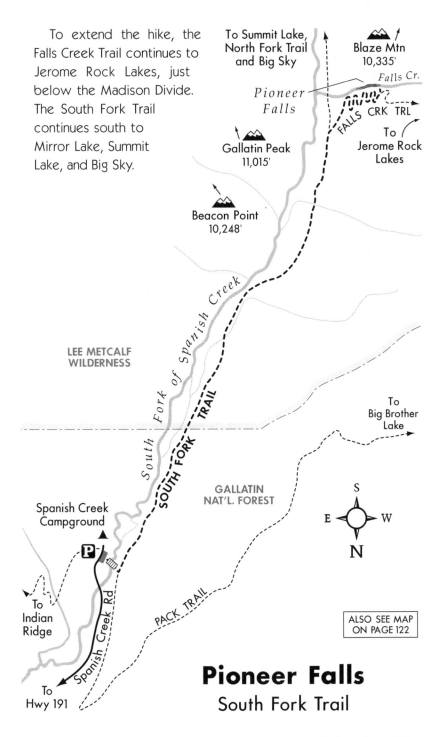

To Summit Lake, North Fork Trail and Big Sky

Blaze Mtn
10,335'

Falls Cr.

Pioneer Falls

FALLS CRK TRL

To Jerome Rock Lakes

Gallatin Peak
11,015'

Beacon Point
10,248'

South Fork of Spanish Creek

LEE METCALF WILDERNESS

SOUTH FORK TRAIL

To Big Brother Lake

Spanish Creek Campground

P

GALLATIN NAT'L. FOREST

S
E · W
N

To Indian Ridge

PACK TRAIL

Spanish Creek Rd

To Hwy 191

ALSO SEE MAP ON PAGE 122

Pioneer Falls
South Fork Trail

49. Hell Roaring Creek Trail

Hiking distance: 5 miles round trip
Hiking time: 2.5 hours
Elevation gain: 500 feet
Maps: U.S.G.S. Garnet Mountain and Beacon Point
  U.S.F.S. Lee Metcalf Wilderness
  Rocky Mountain Surveys: Spanish Peaks

Summary of hike: Hell Roaring Creek, a tributary of the Gallatin River, drains out of Hell Roaring Lake at the head of a steep, narrow drainage between Wilson Peak and Jumbo Mountain in the Spanish Peaks. The Hell Roaring Creek Trail begins at the south end of Beckman Flat, adjacent to the Gallatin River, and climbs past Hell Roaring Lake to Table Mountain. This hike follows the lower portion of the trail, paralleling the creek past a continuous display of tumbling whitewater with small waterfalls, cascades, and pools. The Hell Roaring Creek Trail accesses a network of other backcountry trails within the Spanish Peaks in the Lee Metcalf Wilderness.

Driving directions: From Four Corners 9 miles west of Bozeman, take Highway 191 south towards the Gallatin Canyon. Drive 18.2 miles to the Hell Roaring Creek trailhead parking area on the right, 1.7 miles past Squaw Creek Road.

From Big Sky, the trailhead parking area is 15.5 miles north on Highway 191.

Hiking directions: From the north end of the parking area, head southwest into the forest. A series of switchbacks lead 0.6 miles to a ridge. At the junction midway through the switchbacks, take the hairpin switchback curving left. Once over the ridge, gradually descend to Hell Roaring Creek. Cross the log bridge over the creek, and head southwest up canyon. Continue along the north side of Hell Roaring Creek. At 2.5 miles, enter the Lee Metcalf Wilderness, the turn-around spot for a 5-mile hike.

To hike farther, the trail continues along the creek up to Hell Roaring Lake, Table Mountain, Gallatin Peak, and Summit Lake.

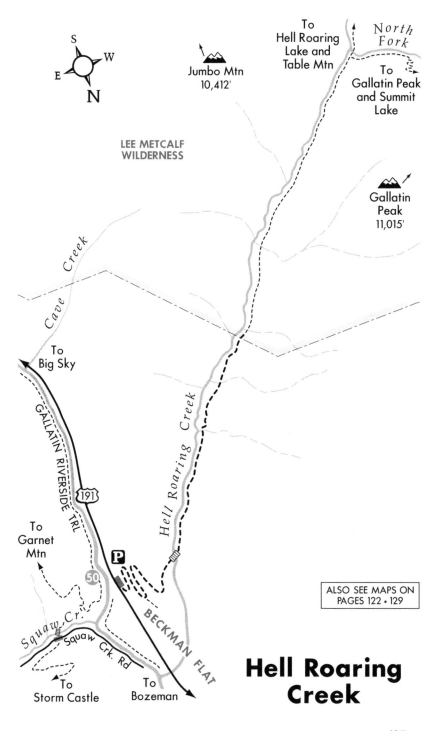

S W E N (compass)

Jumbo Mtn
10,412'

To
Hell Roaring
Lake and
Table Mtn

North Fork

To
Gallatin Peak
and Summit
Lake

LEE METCALF
WILDERNESS

Gallatin
Peak
11,015'

Cave Creek

To
Big Sky

GALLATIN RIVERSIDE TRL.

Hell Roaring Creek

191

To
Garnet
Mtn

50

P

ALSO SEE MAPS ON
PAGES 122 • 129

Squaw Cr.

Squaw Crk. Rd.

BECKMAN FLAT

To
Storm Castle

To
Bozeman

Hell Roaring
Creek

50. Gallatin Riverside Trail

Hiking distance: 5.5 miles round trip
Hiking time: 2.5 hours
Elevation gain: 200 feet
Maps: U.S.G.S. Garnet Mountain
       Rocky Mountain Surveys: Spanish Peaks
       Crystal Bench Maps: Bozeman, Montana

Summary of hike: The Gallatin Riverside Trail parallels the eastern bank of the river on the lower west flank of Garnet Mountain. The trail hugs the rocky cliffs through forests of lodgepole pines, Douglas fir, and Engelmann spruce, passing moss-covered rocks and small streams feeding the river. Kayakers and rafters are often seen working their way downstream. The trailhead is at Squaw Creek at the southern base of Storm Castle. This trail may be hiked as a 2.25-mile, one-way shuttle by leaving a car south of the Highway 191 bridge over the Gallatin River, just beyond the Lava Lake trailhead.

Driving directions: From Four Corners 9 miles west of Bozeman, take Highway 191 south towards the Gallatin Canyon. Drive 16.6 miles to Squaw Creek Road (and Spire Rock Campground) on the left. Turn left, cross Squaw Creek Bridge over the Gallatin River, and curve to the right. Continue 1.8 miles to the trailhead pullouts on both sides of the road.

From Big Sky, Squaw Creek Road is 17.2 miles north on Highway 191.

Hiking directions: The trailhead is on the south side of the road. Cross the bridge over Squaw Creek, and head uphill 0.2 miles through the dense evergreen forest to a signed trail junction. The left fork climbs to Garnet Mountain and a lookout tower. Take the right fork, continuing on the Gallatin Riverside Trail. Zigzag through the forest to a grassy bench on the valley floor. A short distance ahead is a walk-through gate. Walk down to the river's edge. Follow the river bank along the edge of the steep, rocky cliffs, passing talus slopes and limestone outcrops.

The trail ends where the highway crosses the river. Return along the same trail.

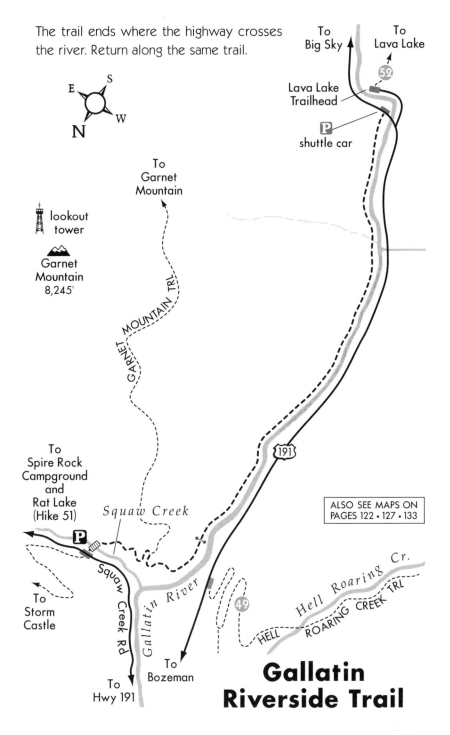

To Big Sky

To Lava Lake

59

Lava Lake Trailhead

P shuttle car

To Garnet Mountain

lookout tower

Garnet Mountain 8,245'

GARNET MOUNTAIN TRL

To Spire Rock Campground and Rat Lake (Hike 51)

Squaw Creek

P

To Storm Castle

Squaw Creek Rd

Gallatin River

191

ALSO SEE MAPS ON PAGES 122 • 127 • 133

Hell Roaring Cr.

HELL ROARING CREEK TRL

49

To Bozeman

To Hwy 191

Gallatin Riverside Trail

51. Rat Lake

Hiking distance: 1.5 miles round trip
Hiking time: 1 hour
Elevation gain: 160 feet
Maps: U.S.G.S. Garnet Mountain
        Rocky Mountain Surveys: Spanish Peaks

map
page 132

Summary of hike: Rat Lake sits on the east slope of Garnet Mountain at 6,600 feet, just south of Squaw Creek. Affectionately named for the rodent, the beautiful, forested lake probably deserves a more attractive title. It is an ideal spot for fishing, picnicking, and strolling, with an easily accessible shoreline. The short, scenic hike is ideal for children. Beyond Rat Lake, the trail continues 1,500 feet up to the Garnet Mountain Lookout Tower.

Driving directions: From Four Corners 9 miles west of Bozeman, take Highway 191 south towards the Gallatin Canyon. Drive 16.6 miles to Squaw Creek Road (and Spire Rock Campground) on the left. Turn left, cross Squaw Creek Bridge over the Gallatin River, and curve to the right. Continue 6.7 miles to the Rat Lake trailhead parking area. Along the way are two road forks—take the right fork both times.

From Big Sky, Squaw Creek Road is 17.2 miles north on Highway 191.

Hiking directions: Take the signed trail south on the old logging road lined with wild lupine. At 0.3 miles is a trail junction. The left fork heads to the Garnet Mountain Lookout Tower. Take the right fork to the north shore of Rat Lake. A trail loops around the wooded shoreline. Return on the same trail.

To continue hiking, the Garnet Mountain Lookout Tower is 3.5 miles from Rat Lake. The trail gains 1,700 feet in elevation up to the summit. Garnet Mountain is also accessible from the Hike 50 trailhead.

52. Cascade Creek to Lava Lake

Hiking distance: 6 miles round trip
Hiking time: 3.5 hours
Elevation gain: 1,600 feet

map
page 133

Maps: U.S.G.S. Garnet Mountain and Hidden Lake
      Rocky Mountain Surveys: Spanish Peaks
      Crystal Bench Maps: Bozeman, Montana

Summary of hike: The tumbling whitewater of Cascade Creek rushes down between Jumbo Mountain and Table Mountain into Lava Lake, a 40-acre tarn formed by a landslide damming the creek. The forest-lined lake sits in a small, steep valley surrounded by granite walls, with the Spanish Peaks rising in the distance. It is the only lake in the Lee Metcalf Wilderness that was not glacially formed. The hike to Lava Lake is among the most popular trails in Gallatin Canyon. The trail begins at the Gallatin River and climbs 1,600 feet along the frothy creek through a thick evergreen forest to the small lake-filled valley. En route, the trail passes turbulent Hoodoo Cascade and a few waterfalls.

Driving directions: From Four Corners 9 miles west of Bozeman, take Highway 191 south towards the Gallatin Canyon. Drive 20.3 miles to the Lava Lake trailhead parking area on the right, just north of the Gallatin River bridge. Turn right and continue 0.2 miles to the parking area.

From Big Sky, the trailhead is 13.5 miles north on Highway 191. From this direction, you can not turn left to access the parking area. Continue to the first turnout and double back.

Hiking directions: Head south on the well-marked trail, immediately gaining elevation in the moist, shady forest. At 0.3 miles, the trail meets Cascade Creek and enters the Lee Metcalf Wilderness. Continue up the canyon, paralleling the noisy creek, and cross a bridge over a tributary stream at one mile. At 1.9 miles, enter a wet meadow. At the upper end of the meadow, cross a log footbridge to the east side of the creek. Climb a series of eight steep switchbacks alongside Hoodoo Cascade.

At just under 3 miles, the path reaches the north end of Lava Lake, with great vistas of Jumbo Mountain, the U-shaped upper valley of Cascade Creek, and Table Mountain. A side path skirts the northwest shoreline to a rocky promontory.

To extend the hike, the main trail zigzags east, climbing more than 2,000 feet to the 9,840-foot summit of Table Mountain in the heart of the Spanish Peaks. Cairns mark the route above timberline.

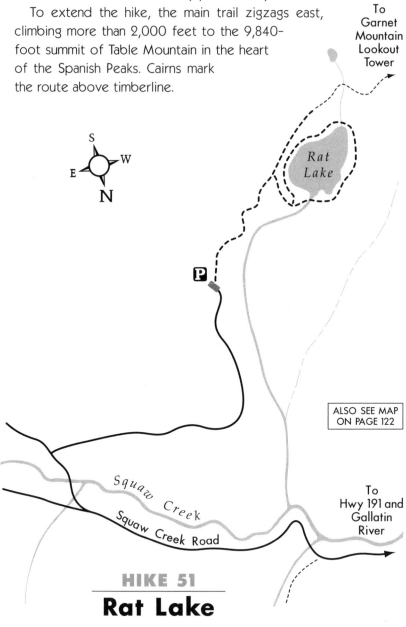

To Garnet Mountain Lookout Tower

S
W
E
N

Rat Lake

P

ALSO SEE MAP
ON PAGE 122

To
Hwy 191 and
Gallatin
River

Squaw Creek

Squaw Creek Road

HIKE 51
Rat Lake

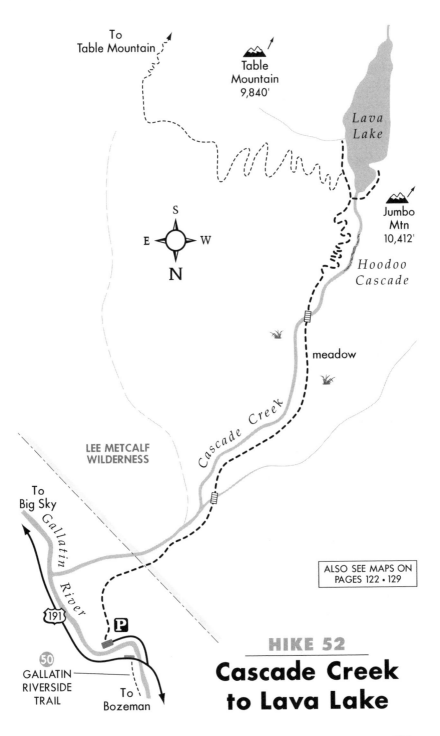

To
Table Mountain

Table
Mountain
9,840'

*Lava
Lake*

S

E · W

N

Jumbo
Mtn
10,412'

*Hoodoo
Cascade*

meadow

Cascade Creek

LEE METCALF
WILDERNESS

To
Big Sky

Gallatin

River

191

ALSO SEE MAPS ON
PAGES 122 · 129

P

50
GALLATIN
RIVERSIDE
TRAIL

To
Bozeman

HIKE 52
Cascade Creek
to Lava Lake

53. Swan Creek Trail

Hiking distance: 1 mile to 10 miles round trip
Hiking time: 30 minutes to 5 hours
Elevation gain: 100 feet to 1,000 feet
Maps: U.S.G.S. Hidden Lake, Garnet Mountain,
      Mount Blackmore, The Sentinel
      Rocky Mountain Surveys: Spanish Peaks
      Crystal Bench Maps: Bozeman, Montana

Summary of hike: The headwaters of Swan Creek begin at 9,400 feet on the upper west slope of Hyalite Peak. The creek drops 3,700 feet to the Gallatin River, tumbling over granite rock and meandering through meadows. The Swan Creek Trail follows the north side of the creek for 11 miles to Hyalite Peak at the Gallatin-Yellowstone Divide, where it connects with the Hyalite Creek Trail (Hike 46) and the Gallatin Divide Trail. This hike follows the lower portion of the trail, passing meadows, beaver ponds, and volcanic rock.

Driving directions: From Four Corners 9 miles west of Bozeman, take Highway 191 south towards the Gallatin Canyon. Drive 24.5 miles to the Swan Creek turnoff on the left. Turn left and continue 1.4 miles alongside Swan Creek to the trailhead parking area at the road's end.

From Big Sky, the Swan Creek turnoff is 9.3 miles north on Highway 191.

Hiking directions: Head east on the wide path along the banks of Swan Creek. The trail quickly narrows to a footpath and enters the forest. Traverse the edge of the hillside while overlooking Swan Creek. At a half mile is a pond on the left, formed by the outlet stream from Lake of the Pines, and a flower-filled meadow. Swan Creek winds through the meadow, pooled up by beaver dams. The trail rises and falls along the hillside, always within view of Swan Creek. Choose your own turn-around spot, and return along the same route.

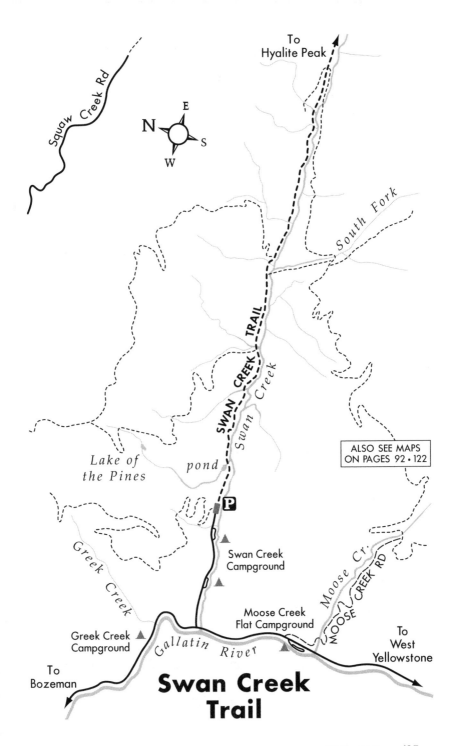

To Hyalite Peak

Squaw Creek Rd

South Fork

N E S W

SWAN CREEK TRAIL

Swan Creek

Lake of the Pines

pond

ALSO SEE MAPS ON PAGES 92 • 122

P

Swan Creek Campground

Moose Cr.

MOOSE CREEK RD

Greek Creek

Moose Creek Flat Campground

Greek Creek Campground

Gallatin River

To West Yellowstone

To Bozeman

Swan Creek Trail

54. Ousel Falls

Hiking distance: 1.6 miles round trip
Hiking time: 45 minutes
Elevation gain: 400 feet
Maps: U.S.G.S. Ousel Falls

Summary of hike: Ousel Falls is a powerful 35-foot cataract that plunges off a moss-covered rock wall onto a granite shelf in an amazing display of whitewater. The waterfall is located in 29-acre Ousel Falls Park a short distance southwest of Big Sky Meadow Village. Ousel Falls is named after water ouzels, small gray birds often present in the nooks next to the waterfall. The interpretive trail parallels the South Fork of the West Fork of the Gallatin River through a forested gulch with three bridge crossings. The trail leads to three separate viewing areas of the falls. Interpretive signs describe the geology, wildlife, and vegetation.

Driving directions: From Four Corners 9 miles west of Bozeman, take Highway 191 south towards the Gallatin Canyon. Drive 33.8 miles to Big Sky Spur Road (Highway 64) at mile marker 48. Turn right and continue 2.9 miles to Ousel Falls Road by the posted Big Sky Town Center. Turn left and continue 1.8 miles to the signed Ousel Falls Park on the left. Turn left and park.

Hiking directions: From the trailhead, the left fork leads two miles to the town center. Take the Yellow Mules Trail to the right, and descend on the wide, gravel path. Enter a Douglas fir forest, and continue on the north wall of the stream-fed canyon. Zigzag down three switchbacks to a bridge crossing over the South Fork of the West Fork of the Gallatin River. Ascend the south wall of the canyon, curving up the mountain contours. Cross a bridge over a tributary stream to a posted Y-fork. The Yellow Mules Trail veers left. Curve right towards Ousel Falls. Descend to the river via two switchbacks. Across the river is a vertical rock wall with seepage dripping through the fractured rock. Walk upstream along the South Fork Cascades and the sandstone formations. Cross a bridge over the river, and climb along the north side of the waterway. Two more switchbacks lead to a 4-way trail split.

The right fork leads a short distance to the South Fork Overlook, with views of the river and falls from high above the river. The second trail to the right leads to the top of Ousel Falls on a natural footpath. The path straight ahead leads to a picnic area and a pool at the base of the waterfall. The left fork leads to a rock overlook of Ousel Falls. Return along the same path.

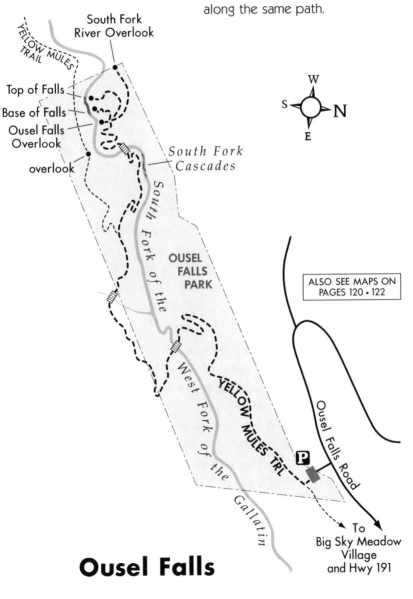

Ousel Falls

55. North Fork Trail

Hiking distance: 6 miles round trip
Hiking time: 3 hours
Elevation gain: 600 feet
Maps: U.S.G.S. Gallatin Peak
      Beartooth Publishing: Bozeman, Big Sky, West Yellowstone
      Rocky Mountain Surveys: Spanish Peaks

map
next page

Summary of hike: The North Fork of the Gallatin River forms in Bear Basin on the south flank of Gallatin Peak, merging with the Middle Fork at Big Sky Meadow Village. The North Fork Trail follows the course of the river upstream into Bear Basin and passes its headwaters to Summit Lake, then descends to the South Fork of Spanish Creek on the opposite side of Gallatin Peak (Hike 48). This is a popular 16-mile overnight backpack trip. This shorter hike takes in the first three miles of the North Fork Trail to a crossing of the river below Mount Chipperfield and Wilson Peak.

Driving directions: From Four Corners 9 miles west of Bozeman, take Highway 191 south towards the Gallatin Canyon. Drive 33.8 miles to Big Sky Spur Road (Highway 64) at mile marker 48. Turn right and continue 4.8 miles to the North Fork Road on the right. Turn right and drive 0.8 miles to the posted trailhead parking area to the left.

Hiking directions: Head north on the wide, well-defined trail. Traverse the east-facing slope, 100 feet above the North Fork of the Gallatin River. Gradually descend and cross a gravel road at 0.6 miles. Continue up the canyon, climbing gradually but steadily. On the right is the North Fork and towering mountains with jagged weather-carved spires, including Wilson Peak and Mount Chipperfield. At 2 miles veer to the right and descend to the log bridge. Cross the bridge over the North Fork of the Gallatin River. Continue along the northeast side of the creek, passing flower-filled meadows, pockets of evergreens, and a series of cascades and small waterfalls formed by downfall logs. Climb a small rise to a posted junction at 3 miles. This is the turn-around spot.

To extend the hike, the North Fork Trail steadily climbs over 2 miles into Bear Basin while gaining 1,200 feet. After the basin, the trail steeply ascends the Spanish Peaks 3 more miles to Summit Lake at 9,500 feet, connecting to a network of trails.

Hike 56 continues on the left fork—the North Fork Tie Trail. This route crosses back over the creek and climbs to the ridge, forming an 8.4-mile loop via the Ridge Trail.

56. North Fork—Ridge Trail Loop

Hiking distance: 8.4 mile loop
Hiking time: 4 hours
Elevation gain: 1,200 feet

map
next page

Maps: U.S.G.S. Gallatin Peak and Lone Mountain
Beartooth Publishing: Bozeman, Big Sky, W.Yellowstone
Rocky Mountain Surveys: Spanish Peaks

Summary of hike: This hike continues from Hike 55, forming an 8.4-mile loop up through a river drainage and back down across a ridge. The trail follows the North Fork of the Gallatin River for the first three miles (Hike 55), crossing two bridges over the creek. The North Fork Tie Trail (this hike) continues up the west canyon wall to the ridge between Beehive Basin and the North Fork drainage. The hike then returns down the Ridge Trail, offering views of Lone Mountain, Gallatin Peak, the Spanish Peaks, and Bear Basin.

Driving directions: Same as Hike 55.

Hiking directions: Follow the hiking directions for Hike 55 to the posted junction at 3 miles. Bear left on the North Fork Tie Trail, and descend to the North Fork of the Gallatin River. Cross the one-log bridge and head up the hillside. Climb a series of 11 switchbacks, with an awesome vista of Bear Basin, Gallatin Peak, the jagged spine of the Spanish Peaks, and the North Fork drainage. Continue climbing to the ridge. Follow the ridge north and curve west through a tree-rimmed meadow to a junction by the unpaved Ridge Road. The right fork leads to Beehive Basin (Hike 57). Bear left on the Ridge Trail. Cross and recross the dirt road, following the Ridge Trail signs. Descend through the forest and skirt the ridge, with alternating views of Beehive Basin and the North Fork Canyon. Descend the west wall of the North Fork drainage, and steadily descend to the Ridge Road. Bear left on the forested dirt road, and continue 1.7 miles downhill, completing the loop at the trailhead.

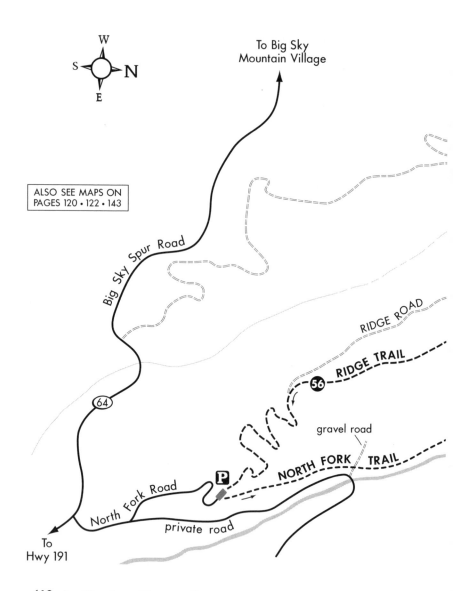

To Big Sky
Mountain Village

W
S ✛ N
E

ALSO SEE MAPS ON
PAGES 120 • 122 • 143

Big Sky Spur Road

RIDGE ROAD

RIDGE TRAIL

56

gravel road

64

NORTH FORK TRAIL

P

North Fork Road

private road

To
Hwy 191

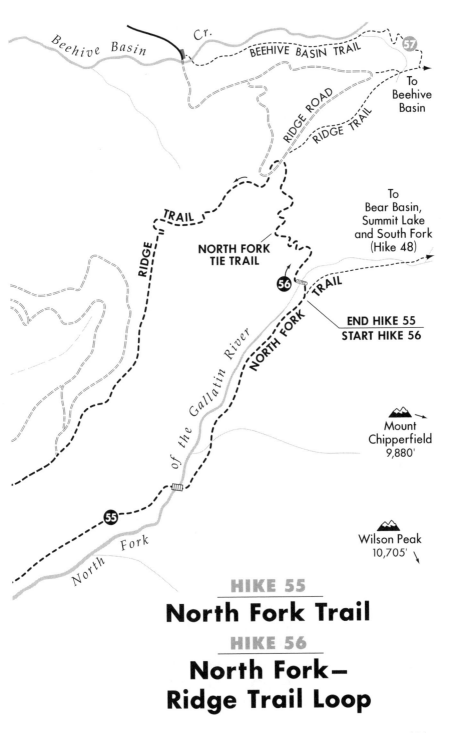

Beehive Basin Cr.

BEEHIVE BASIN TRAIL

57

To Beehive Basin

RIDGE ROAD

RIDGE TRAIL

TRAIL

RIDGE

NORTH FORK
TIE TRAIL

To
Bear Basin,
Summit Lake
and South Fork
(Hike 48)

56

TRAIL

NORTH FORK

of the Gallatin River

END HIKE 55
START HIKE 56

Mount
Chipperfield
9,880'

55

North Fork

Wilson Peak
10,705'

HIKE 55

North Fork Trail

HIKE 56

North Fork–
Ridge Trail Loop

57. Beehive Basin Trail

Hiking distance: 6.5 miles round trip
Hiking time: 4 hours
Elevation gain: 1,200 feet
Maps: U.S.G.S. Lone Mountain
      Beartooth Publishing: Bozeman, Big Sky, West Yellowstone
      Rocky Mountain Surveys: Spanish Peaks

Summary of hike: Beehive Basin sits in a bowl surrounded on three sides by 10,000-foot mountains in the Spanish Peaks Primitive Area. The picturesque basin is a glacial cirque with a small lake. The lake sits at 9,200 feet beneath the rock walls of Blaze Mountain, Gallatin Peak, and Mount Chipperfield. This top-of-the-world hike includes alpine meadows covered with wildflowers, tall stands of evergreens, and a tumbling creek. At trail's end is an unnamed lake and wide open vistas into the Lee Metcalf Wilderness. Moose frequent the area.

Driving directions: From Four Corners 9 miles west of Bozeman, take Highway 191 south towards the Gallatin Canyon. Drive 33.8 miles to Big Sky Spur Road (Highway 64) at mile marker 48. Turn right and continue 10.1 miles to Beehive Basin Road on the right. (It is located 1.3 miles beyond the Big Sky Mountain Village turnoff and 30 yards before the Moonlight Basin Ranch entrance.) Turn right and drive 1.6 miles to the posted trailhead parking area on the left.

Hiking directions: Walk north to Beehive Creek. Cross a two-log bridge over the creek, and head up the grassy meadow rimmed with evergreens. Cross the east slope of the meadow, overlooking the serpentine creek and Blaze Mountain on the jagged ridge of the Spanish Peaks. Cross a fork of the creek, and zigzag up three switchbacks on the open slope. The vistas extend down canyon to pyramid-shaped Lone Mountain and the Madison Range. The path reaches a posted T-junction at one mile. The right fork leads two miles to the North Fork Trail (Hike 55). Bear left into a large meadow and three creek crossings. After the third crossing, begin a second ascent to another meadow and a pond, passing limestone rock formations. After crossing the second meadow, begin the final ascent. The trail flattens out at a crescent-shaped lake in a cirque, surrounded by a grassy basin marbled with streams. The views are breathtaking. Return on the same trail.

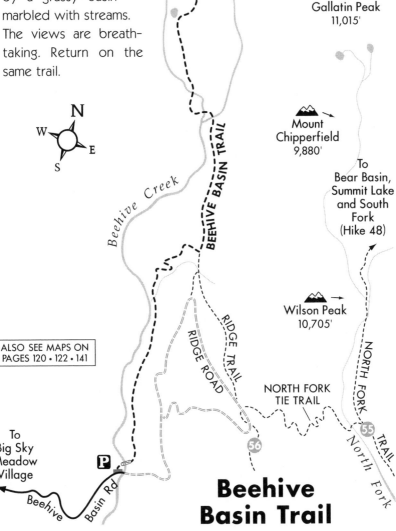

Blaze Mtn
10,384'

LEE METCALF
WILDERNESS

Gallatin Peak
11,015'

Mount
Chipperfield
9,880'

To
Bear Basin,
Summit Lake
and South
Fork
(Hike 48)

Wilson Peak
10,705'

BEEHIVE BASIN TRAIL

Beehive Creek

N
W E
S

ALSO SEE MAPS ON
PAGES 120 • 122 • 141

RIDGE ROAD

RIDGE TRAIL

NORTH FORK
TIE TRAIL

NORTH FORK TRAIL

56

55

North Fork

To
Big Sky
Meadow
Village

P

Beehive Basin Rd

Beehive
Basin Trail

58. Porcupine Creek

Hiking distance: 4 miles round trip
Hiking time: 2 hours
Elevation gain: 240 feet
Maps: U.S.G.S. Lone Indian Peak

Summary of hike: The Porcupine Creek Trail begins near the Gallatin River and climbs 9 miles up to its headwaters in Onion Basin at the Gallatin-Yellowstone Divide. En route, the trail gains more than 3,000 feet to the basin and ridge in the Gallatin Petrified Forest. Connecting trails lead to Eaglehead Mountain, Fortress Mountain, and into the Rock Creek drainage in Paradise Valley. This easy hike follows the first two miles of the creek into the Porcupine Elk Preserve. The large, rolling meadows are a vital winter range for elk and home to many coyotes. After the snow melts, moose and deer are frequently spotted in the meadows.

Driving directions: From Four Corners 9 miles west of Bozeman, take Highway 191 south towards the Gallatin Canyon. Drive 36.5 miles to the Porcupine Creek turnoff on the left (2.7 miles south of the Big Sky turnoff). Turn left (east) and drive 0.5 miles, passing the log cabins to the trailhead. Park along the road.

Hiking directions: The trailhead is to the left of the road. Cross the footbridge over Porcupine Creek and head upstream. Parallel the creek through open sage brush meadows dotted with pine trees. At one mile, cross Porcupine Creek. To avoid wading across, walk back downstream about 50 yards to a solid log crossing. Once over the creek, take the narrow footpath that rejoins the main trail. Within 50 feet is another junction. Take the left fork and ascend the 200-foot slope. On the ridge, Porcupine Creek can be seen placidly flowing through a large open meadow. Descend into the meadow to a posted junction. This is the turn-around spot.

To continue hiking, take the trail to the left. Cross Porcupine Creek and the meadow. The trail heads up the ridge, crosses First Creek, then loops back, adding two miles to the hike.

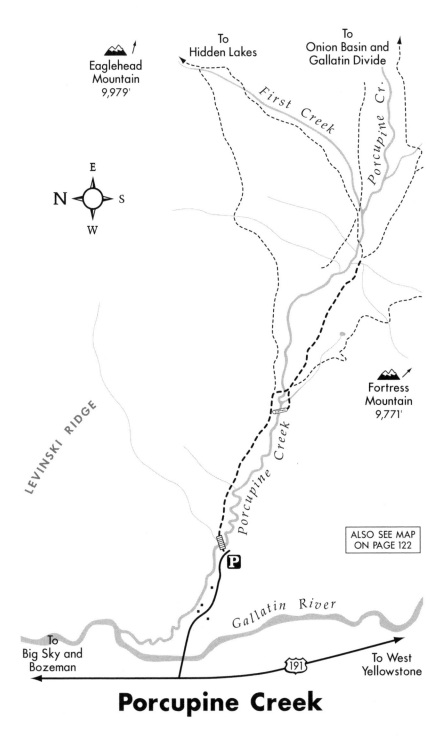

To Hidden Lakes

To Onion Basin and Gallatin Divide

Eaglehead Mountain 9,979'

First Creek

Porcupine Cr.

N E S W

LEVINSKI RIDGE

Fortress Mountain 9,771'

Porcupine Creek

ALSO SEE MAP ON PAGE 122

P

Gallatin River

To Big Sky and Bozeman

191

To West Yellowstone

Porcupine Creek

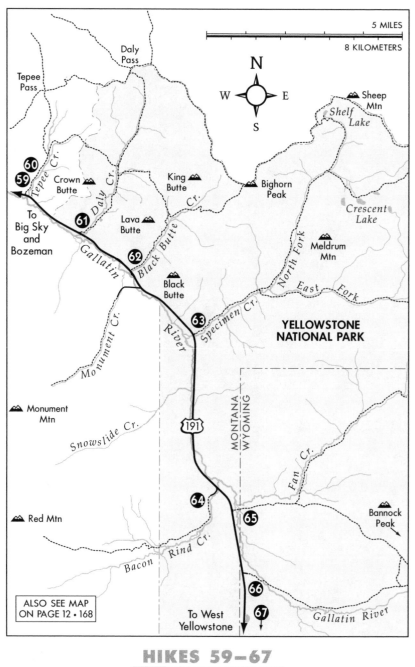

5 MILES

8 KILOMETERS

Daly Pass

Tepee Pass

Sheep Mtn

Shelf Lake

N
W   E
S

60
59

Crown Butte

King Butte

Bighorn Peak

Crescent Lake

61

Lava Butte

Black Butte Cr.

To Big Sky and Bozeman

Gallatin

62

Black Butte

North Fork

Meldrum Mtn

East Fork

63

Specimen Cr.

YELLOWSTONE NATIONAL PARK

Monument Cr.

River

Monument Mtn

Snowslide Cr.

191

MONTANA
WYOMING

Fan Cr.

Red Mtn

64

65

Bannock Peak

Bacon Rind Cr.

ALSO SEE MAP ON PAGE 12 • 168

To West Yellowstone

66

67

Gallatin River

HIKES 59–67

Yellowstone from the Gallatin

Yellowstone National Park from the Upper Gallatin Valley

HIKES 59—67

The headwaters of the Gallatin River begin from the northwest corner of Yellowstone National Park. The area is filled with verdant valleys, alpine meadows, and crystal clear streams fed by alpine springs and snowmelt. These hikes branch off from the Gallatin River and climb up stream-fed valleys surrounded by the peaks of the Gallatin and Madison Ranges. All of the trails in this remote region of the park follow creeks through open, grassy slopes with rock escarpments and forests of aspen, Douglas fir, and lodgepole pine. The trails interconnect with the Hebgen Lake area, the Madison Range, the northern end of the Gallatin Range to Bozeman, Paradise Valley, and to Mammoth in the park.

Hikes 59—63 head northeast along three upper tributaries of the Gallatin. The trails eventually connect with Skyline Ridge, which forms the northwest Yellowstone Park boundary. The hikes take in the first 2—4 miles of the trails along quiet, gentle inclines, but the hikes can easily be extended for a longer outing.

The Bacon Rind Trail—Hike 64—is the only hike in Yellowstone that enters the Madison Range to the west and connects with the Lee Metcalf Wilderness. The lush valleys just north of the Madison River are included in Hikes 65—67.

The vast, open terrain and sweeping landscape throughout this region offers great scenery. The wildlife is abundant, including bear, moose, elk, and many species of birds.

59. Tepee Creek Trail to Tepee Pass

Hiking distance: 6 miles round trip
Hiking time: 3 hours
Elevation gain: 900 feet
Maps: U.S.G.S. Sunshine Point

Summary of hike: The Tepee Creek Trail follows the watercourse of Tepee Creek through expansive grasslands to Tepee Pass at the head of the verdant valley. From the pass are tremendous sweeping views down the wide valley and beyond, from the Madison Range to the Gallatin Range.

Driving directions: From Four Corners 9 miles west of Bozeman, take Highway 191 south towards the Gallatin Canyon. Drive 49.8 miles (16 miles south of the Big Sky turnoff) to the signed trail on the left by mile marker 32. Turn left and park 100 yards ahead by the trailhead.

From West Yellowstone, the trailhead is 33 miles north on Highway 191.

Hiking directions: Head northeast up the wide grassy draw between Sunshine Point and Crown Butte. Follow the trail along Tepee Creek to a signed junction with the Tepee Creek Cutoff Trail at 1.1 miles. The right fork crosses Tepee Creek and leads eastward into Yellowstone (Hike 60). Take the left fork towards Tepee Pass and Buffalo Horn Divide. Climb a small hill, then traverse the hillside above the valley. Continue past the prominent Grouse Mountain and stands of aspens and pines. After numerous dips and rises along the rolling ridges, the trail begins a half-mile ascent to Tepee Pass. At the top of the valley, near a dense stand of evergreens, is a signed 4-way junction on Tepee Pass. The right fork leads 200 yards to a flat area above the saddle with great views. This is the turn-around spot.

To hike farther, the east trail continues two miles to the Yellowstone National Park boundary, then on to Daly Pass. The north trail from Tepee Pass descends for 2.5 miles to Buffalo Horn Creek. The west trail from Tepee Pass leads down Wilson Draw to the Gallatin River.

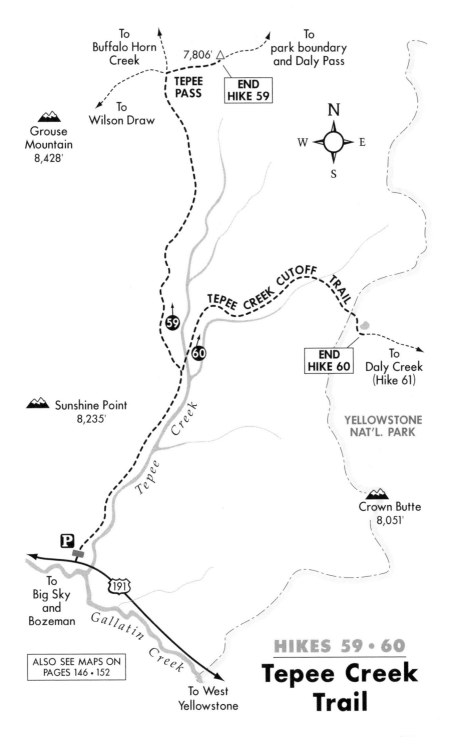

To Buffalo Horn Creek

7,806'

To park boundary and Daly Pass

TEPEE PASS

END HIKE 59

To Wilson Draw

Grouse Mountain 8,428'

N
W E
S

TEPEE CREEK CUTOFF TRAIL

59

60

END HIKE 60

To Daly Creek (Hike 61)

Sunshine Point 8,235'

YELLOWSTONE NAT'L. PARK

Tepee Creek

Crown Butte 8,051'

P

To Big Sky and Bozeman

191

Gallatin Creek

ALSO SEE MAPS ON PAGES 146 • 152

To West Yellowstone

HIKES 59 • 60
Tepee Creek Trail

60. Tepee Creek Trail to the Yellowstone National Park boundary

Hiking distance: 4.6 miles round trip
Hiking time: 2.5 hours
Elevation gain: 700 feet
Maps: U.S.G.S. Sunshine Point

map
page 149

Summary of hike: The Tepee Creek Trail begins just outside the northwest corner of Yellowstone National Park. The trail crosses gentle slopes through a broad grassy valley surrounded by mountains and dense tree-lined ridges. The hike ends on a grassy ridgetop at the Yellowstone boundary overlooking the Daly Creek drainage, the next drainage to the east (Hike 61).

Driving directions: Same as Hike 59.

Hiking directions: Hike northeast past the hitching posts, and cross the grassy slopes along the base of Sunshine Point. Follow the open expanse along the west side of Tepee Creek to a signed junction with the Tepee Creek Cutoff Trail at 1.1 miles. The left fork heads north to Tepee Pass and Buffalo Horn Creek (Hike 59). Take the right fork across Tepee Creek, and continue up the hillside on the east side of the creek. The trail curves to the right and heads east up a narrow drainage surrounded by mountains and tree groves. Near the top of a meadow, follow the ridge to the signed Yellowstone boundary on the saddle. Just below the saddle is a pond. After enjoying the views, return along the same route.

To hike farther, the trail descends to Daly Creek in Yellowstone Park (Hike 61).

61. Daly Creek Trail

Hiking distance: 5.2 miles round trip
Hiking time: 2.5 hours
Elevation gain: 350 feet
Maps: U.S.G.S. Sunshine Point and Big Horn Peak
　　　　Trails Illustrated: Mammoth Hot Springs

map
page 152

Summary of hike: Daly Creek is the northernmost drainage in Yellowstone National Park. This backcountry hike makes a gradual ascent up the scenic valley, crossing the rolling meadows and open hillsides parallel to Daly Creek. The hillsides are fringed with aspens and Douglas fir. The impressive Crown Butte, Lava Butte, and King Butte formations are prominent throughout the hike. To the northeast is the Sky Rim Ridge that forms the northeast boundary of Yellowstone.

Driving directions: From Four Corners 9 miles west of Bozeman, take Highway 191 south towards the Gallatin Canyon. Drive 51.4 miles (17.6 miles south of the Big Sky turnoff) to the signed trail on the left between mile markers 30 and 31. Turn left and park in the lot.

From West Yellowstone, the trailhead is 31.4 miles north on Highway 191.

Hiking directions: Head northeast, skirting around the right side of the embankment parallel to Daly Creek. At a quarter mile, cross the log footbridge over Daly Creek. To the north, on the Yellowstone Park boundary, is the Crown Butte formation. King Butte rises high in the northeast. Climb the rolling ridge along the east side of the drainage through stands of lodgepole pines. Watch for a vernal pool on the right. At one mile, the trail climbs a small hill and crosses a couple of streams to a great profile view of Crown Butte, now to the west. Continue through the open meadows past a signed junction with the Black Butte Cutoff Trail on the right at 1.8 miles. The well-defined trail straight ahead reaches the Tepee Creek Cutoff Trail junction at 2.6 miles. This is the turn-around point.

To hike farther, the north trail (straight ahead) climbs three additional miles to Daly Pass at the park's northern boundary on Sky Rim Ridge. The left fork heads west, over the ridge and into the Tepee Creek valley (Hikes 59 and 60). The Black Butte Cutoff Trail heads over the ridge to the east to the Black Butte Creek drainage—Hike 62.

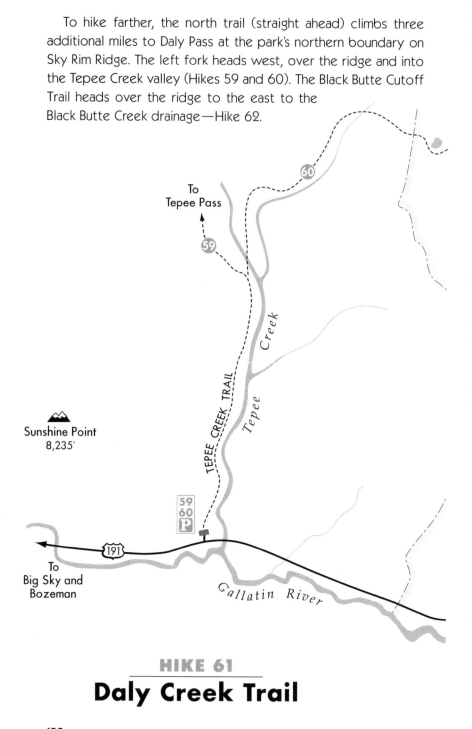

HIKE 61
Daly Creek Trail

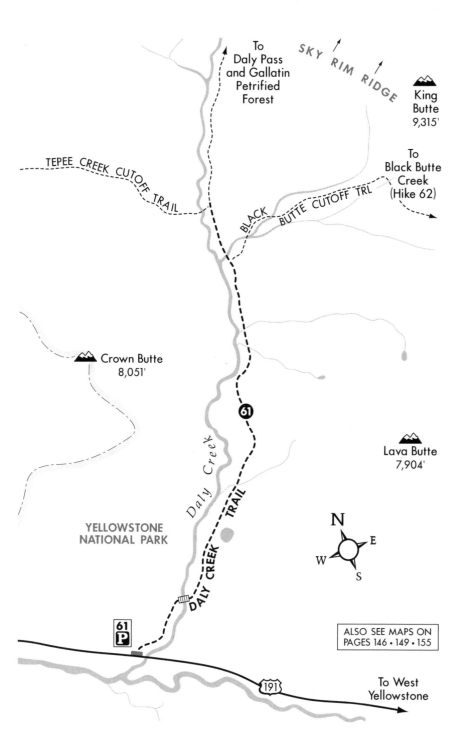

To
Daly Pass
and Gallatin
Petrified
Forest

SKY RIM RIDGE

King
Butte
9,315'

TEPEE CREEK CUTOFF TRAIL

BLACK BUTTE CUTOFF TRL

To
Black Butte
Creek
(Hike 62)

Crown Butte
8,051'

61

Lava Butte
7,904'

Daly Creek

DALY CREEK TRAIL

YELLOWSTONE
NATIONAL PARK

N
E
W
S

61
P

ALSO SEE MAPS ON
PAGES 146 • 149 • 155

191

To West
Yellowstone

62. Black Butte Creek Trail

Hiking distance: 4 miles round trip
Hiking time: 2 hours
Elevation gain: 600 feet
Maps: U.S.G.S. Big Horn Peak
Trails Illustrated: Mammoth Hot Springs

Summary of hike: The Black Butte Creek Trail begins at the base of Black Butte in the Gallatin Valley. The trail parallels Black Butte Creek up a beautiful forested drainage to a meadow at the base of King Butte. The narrow valley has aspen, lodgepole pine, and Douglas fir. This trail is an access route up to Big Horn Peak, Shelf Lake, and the summit of Sheep Mountain.

Driving directions: From Four Corners 9 miles west of Bozeman, take Highway 191 south towards the Gallatin Canyon. Drive 53 miles (19.2 miles south of the Big Sky turnoff) to the signed trail on the left. Park on the right, 50 yards south of the signed trail, in the parking area between mile markers 28 and 29.

From West Yellowstone, the trailhead is 29.8 miles north on Highway 191.

Hiking directions: Cross the highway to the signed trail on the north side of Black Butte Creek. Hike up the forested draw between Black Butte and Lava Butte. Head gradually uphill, following the creek through meadows and pine groves along the creek drainage. Meander across the various slopes and rolling hills while remaining close to Black Butte Creek. At 1.5 miles, the trail enters a dense, old growth lodgepole forest. After a quarter mile, the path breaks out into an open meadow. King Butte and Big Horn Peak tower above to the northeast. At two miles, in the meadow at the base of King Butte, is a signed trail junction. This is the turn-around spot.

To hike farther, the left (northwest) fork leads 2.1 miles to Daly Creek (Hike 61). The right (east) fork crosses the meadow along Black Butte Creek. After crossing the creek, the trail begins a steep 5-mile ascent to the summit of Bighorn Peak and on to Shelf Lake.

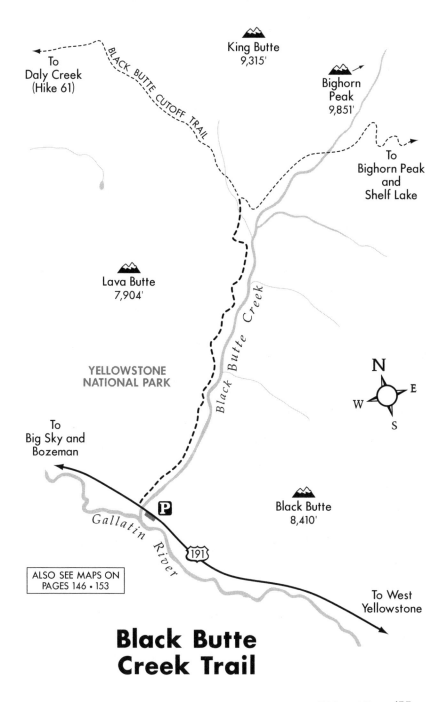

To
Daly Creek
(Hike 61)

BLACK BUTTE CUTOFF TRAIL

King Butte
9,315'

Bighorn
Peak
9,851'

To
Bighorn Peak
and
Shelf Lake

Lava Butte
7,904'

Black Butte Creek

YELLOWSTONE
NATIONAL PARK

N
W   E
S

To
Big Sky and
Bozeman

P

Black Butte
8,410'

Gallatin River

191

To West
Yellowstone

ALSO SEE MAPS ON
PAGES 146 • 153

Black Butte
Creek Trail

63. Specimen Creek Trail

Hiking distance: 4.2 miles round trip
Hiking time: 2 hours
Elevation gain: 240 feet
Maps: U.S.G.S. Big Horn Peak
          Trails Illustrated: Mammoth Hot Springs

Summary of hike: The nearly flat Specimen Creek Trail follows Specimen Creek up the canyon through a mature forest dominated by lodgepole pines. This beautiful drainage crosses bridges over feeder streams to an open meadow at the confluence of the North Fork and East Fork of Specimen Creek. The meadow is frequented by elk and moose.

Driving directions: From Four Corners 9 miles west of Bozeman, take Highway 191 south towards the Gallatin Canyon. Drive 55.3 miles (21.5 miles south of the Big Sky turnoff) to the signed trail on the left between mile markers 25 and 26. Turn left and park by the trailhead 30 yards ahead.

From West Yellowstone, the trailhead is 27.5 miles north on Highway 191.

Hiking directions: Head east along Specimen Creek through the lodgepole pine forest. Pass talus slopes on the northern side of the narrow drainage. As the canyon widens, the trail alternates between lush stands of pines and open meadows. At 1.3 miles, cross a footbridge over a stream. Traverse the forested hillside to another footbridge over a stream to a signed trail split at two miles. The right fork follows the Sportsman Lake Trail to High Lake and Sportsman Lake, 6 and 8 miles ahead. Take the Specimen Creek Trail to the left. Within minutes is campsite WE1. The campsite sits in an open meadow by Specimen Creek, which meanders through the meadow. A short distance ahead is the confluence of the North Fork and the East Fork, the turn-around spot.

To hike farther, the trail continues up to the headwaters of the North Fork at Crescent Lake and Shelf Lake, an additional 5 miles ahead.

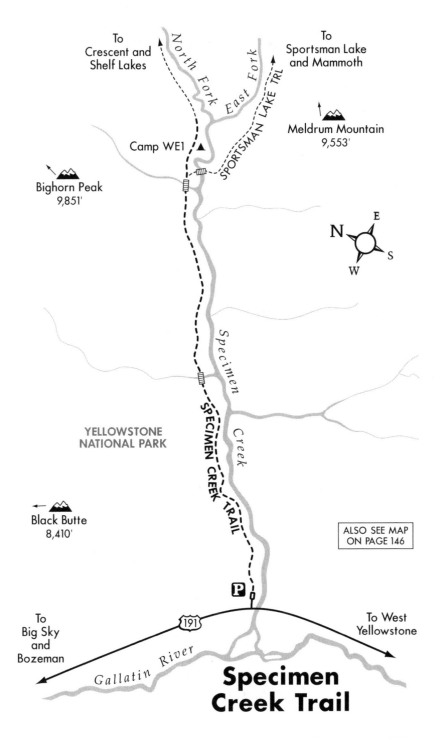

To Crescent and Shelf Lakes

North Fork

East Fork

To Sportsman Lake and Mammoth

SPORTSMAN LAKE TRL

Camp WE1 ▲

Meldrum Mountain
9,553'

Bighorn Peak
9,851'

N E S W

YELLOWSTONE
NATIONAL PARK

Specimen   Creek

SPECIMEN CREEK TRAIL

Black Butte
8,410'

ALSO SEE MAP
ON PAGE 146

P

To Big Sky and Bozeman

191

To West Yellowstone

Gallatin River

Specimen Creek Trail

64. Bacon Rind Creek Trail

Hiking distance: 4.2 miles round trip
Hiking time: 2 hours
Elevation gain: 200 feet
Maps: U.S.G.S. Divide Lake
　　　　 Trails Illustrated: Mammoth Hot Springs

Summary of hike: The Bacon Rind Creek Trail is the only hike inside Yellowstone that heads west from the Gallatin Valley. The flat, easy trail parallels the meandering Bacon Rind Creek through a valley surrounded by high mountain peaks. Moose, elk, and grizzly bears frequent the meadow. Beyond the western park boundary, the trail enters the Lee Metcalf Wilderness in the Gallatin National Forest.

Driving directions: From Four Corners 9 miles west of Bozeman, take Highway 191 south towards the Gallatin Canyon. Drive 59.3 miles (25.5 miles south of the Big Sky turnoff) to the trailhead sign on the right between mile markers 22 and 23. Turn right on the unpaved road, and drive 0.3 miles to the parking area.

From West Yellowstone, the trailhead is 23.5 miles north on Highway 191.

Hiking directions: Head south past the trail sign along the north side of Bacon Rind Creek. Follow the drainage upstream through beautiful stands of pine and fir. The path remains close to the riparian watercourse for the first 0.7 miles, where the valley opens to the Gallatin River. Bacon Rind Creek flows placidly through the wide valley between the forested hillsides. Continue up the draw to the head of the valley and cross a stream. Evergreens enclose the top of the meadow at the signed Yellowstone National Park boundary. This is the turn-around point. To return, reverse your route.

To hike farther, the trail enters the Lee Metcalf Wilderness, crosses Migration Creek, and eventually ascends to Monument Mountain (8 miles from the park boundary) and Cone Peak (7 miles from the park boundary).

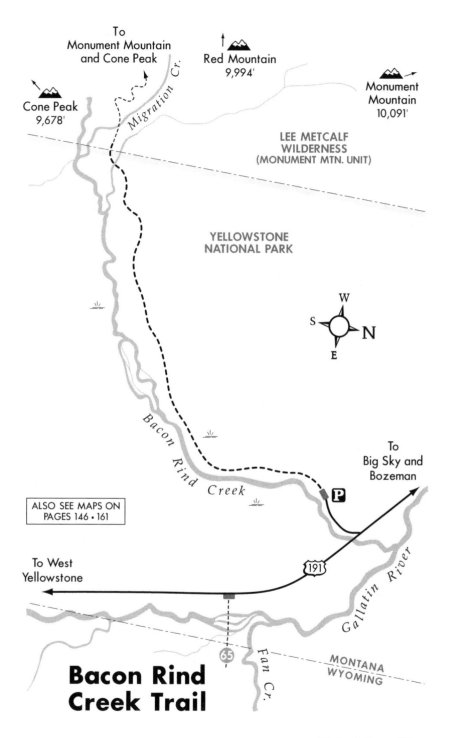

To
Monument Mountain
and Cone Peak

Red Mountain
9,994'

Monument
Mountain
10,091'

Cone Peak
9,678'

Migration Cr.

LEE METCALF
WILDERNESS
(MONUMENT MTN. UNIT)

YELLOWSTONE
NATIONAL PARK

W
S ✦ N
E

Bacon Rind Creek

To
Big Sky and
Bozeman

P

ALSO SEE MAPS ON
PAGES 146 • 161

To West
Yellowstone

191

Gallatin River

65

Fan Cr.

MONTANA
WYOMING

Bacon Rind
Creek Trail

65. Fawn Pass Trail to Fan Creek

Hiking distance: 3 miles round trip
Hiking time: 1.5 hours
Elevation gain: 200 feet
Maps: U.S.G.S. Divide Lake
       Trails Illustrated: Mammoth Hot Springs

Summary of hike: The Fawn Pass Trail to Fan Creek is an easy hike through forested rolling hills and scenic meadows. The Fan Creek Trail (not shown on the U.S.G.S. map) is a fishing access trail established in the early 1980s. From the junction with the Fawn Pass Trail, the Fan Creek Trail heads northeast along the creek through Fan Creek meadow. Moose and elk frequent this beautiful meadow.

Driving directions: From Four Corners 9 miles west of Bozeman, take Highway 191 south towards the Gallatin Canyon. Drive 60 miles (26.2 miles south of the Big Sky turnoff) to the signed trail on the left, just south of mile marker 22. Turn left and park in the trailhead parking area.

From West Yellowstone, the trailhead is 22.8 miles north on Highway 191.

Hiking directions: Head east down a short flight of steps on the Fawn Pass Trail. After the trail register, cross the meadow marbled with meandering streams that form the upper Gallatin River. A series of wooden footbridges cross the various lucid streams. Ascend the slope and enter the forested hillside. Cross the gently rolling hills to a signed trail split at 1.4 miles. The Fawn Pass Trail bears right to the Bighorn Pass Cutoff Trail and Fawn Pass. Take the Fan Creek Trail to the left. The trail descends into the wide open meadow to Fan Creek. At the creek is a wonderful picnic spot and place to rest.

To hike farther, the trail follows Fan Creek through the mountain valley for another 6 miles to the Sportsman Lake Trail, wading across Fan Creek three times.

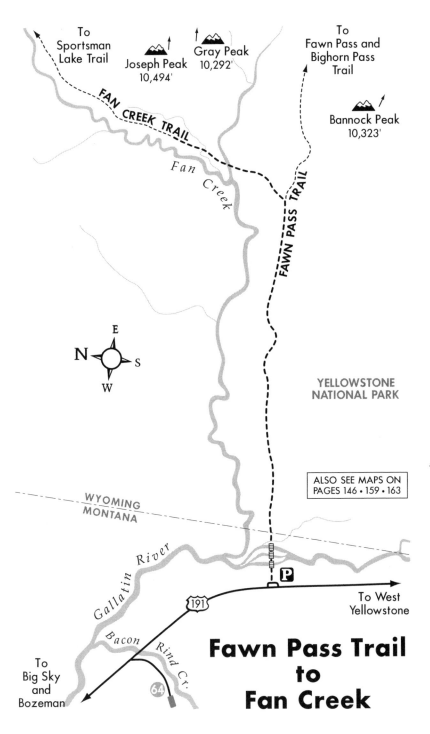

To
Sportsman
Lake Trail

Joseph Peak
10,494'

Gray Peak
10,292'

To
Fawn Pass and
Bighorn Pass
Trail

Bannock Peak
10,323'

FAN CREEK TRAIL

Fan Creek

FAWN PASS TRAIL

N E S W

YELLOWSTONE
NATIONAL PARK

ALSO SEE MAPS ON
PAGES 146 • 159 • 163

WYOMING
MONTANA

Gallatin River

P

To West
Yellowstone

191

Bacon Rind Cr.

To
Big Sky
and
Bozeman

64

Fawn Pass Trail
to
Fan Creek

66. Bighorn Pass Trail along the Upper Gallatin River

Hiking distance: 1 to 12 miles round trip
Hiking time: Variable
Elevation gain: 150 feet
Maps: U.S.G.S. Divide Lake and Joseph Peak
Trails Illustrated: Mammoth Hot Springs

Summary of hike: The Upper Gallatin Valley is a vast, open meadow that stretches along the Upper Gallatin River for many miles, making it easy to choose your own hiking distance. The relaxing hike through the scenic, treeless valley offers excellent trout fishing and wildlife viewing. The trail eventually leads over Bighorn Pass and Bannock Peak, which can be seen looming in the distance at the end of the valley. The headwaters of the Gallatin River begin at Gallatin Lake just south of the pass.

Driving directions: From Four Corners 9 miles west of Bozeman, take Highway 191 south towards the Gallatin Canyon. Drive 61.5 miles (27.7 miles south of the Big Sky turnoff) to the signed trail on the left between mile markers 20 and 21. Turn left and drive 0.2 miles to the parking area.

From West Yellowstone, the trailhead is 21.3 miles north on Highway 191.

Hiking directions: Take the trail southeast past the hitching posts and trail sign along the west edge of the Gallatin River. Walk through the stands of lodgepole pines, heading upstream along the winding river. At a quarter mile, cross the log bridge over the river. Continue southeast on the well-defined path. Follow the river through the broad, grassy meadows while enjoying the spectacular views of the Gallatin Valley stretching to the east. Turn around at any point along the trail. Bighorn Pass is 12 miles from the trailhead.

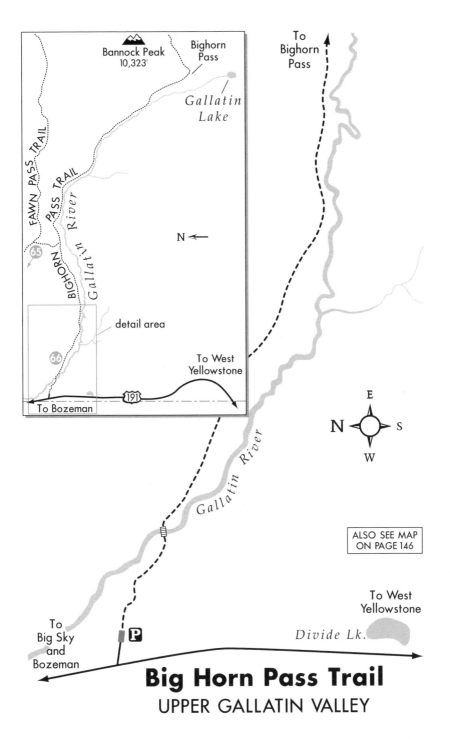

Bannock Peak
10,323'

Bighorn
Pass

To
Bighorn
Pass

*Gallatin
Lake*

FAWN PASS TRAIL

PASS TRAIL

BIGHORN

Gallatin River

65

N ←

detail area

66

To West
Yellowstone

191

To Bozeman

E

N ⬥ S

W

Gallatin River

ALSO SEE MAP
ON PAGE 146

To West
Yellowstone

Divide Lk.

P

To
Big Sky
and
Bozeman

Big Horn Pass Trail
UPPER GALLATIN VALLEY

67. Gneiss Creek Trail from the Gallatin

Hiking distance: 3.6 miles round trip
Hiking time: 2 hours
Elevation gain: 300 feet
Maps: U.S.G.S. Richards Creek
Trails Illustrated: Mammoth Hot Springs

Summary of hike: This hike follows the first section of the Gneiss Creek Trail from the northwest trailhead in the Gallatin. The 14-mile trail leads through the Madison Valley, crossing several creeks en route to the southern trailhead at the Madison River bridge (see inset map). This hike is an easy walk through the beautiful open terrain to Campanula Creek, a tributary of Gneiss Creek. The valley is abundant with wildlife.

Driving directions: From Four Corners 9 miles west of Bozeman, take Highway 191 south towards the Gallatin Canyon. Drive 72.2 miles (38.4 miles south of the Big Sky turnoff) to the signed trail on the left between mile markers 9 and 10. Turn left and park in the area straight ahead, past Fir Ridge Cemetery.

From West Yellowstone, the trailhead is 10.6 miles north on Highway 191.

Hiking directions: Follow the old, grassy two-track road east through aspen and pine groves. Cross a small rise and parallel the signed Yellowstone Park boundary. At 0.3 miles, the trail enters the park at a sign-in register. Continue along the ridge above Duck Creek and Richards Creek to the south. Head east along the rolling hills. The trail gradually loses elevation past the forested slopes of Sandy Butte to the right. At the east end of Sandy Butte, descend into the draw to Campanula Creek. Follow the creek upstream a short distance to the creek crossing, the turn-around point for this hike.

To hike farther, cross the creek and continue southeast through the open, flat valley along Gneiss Creek.

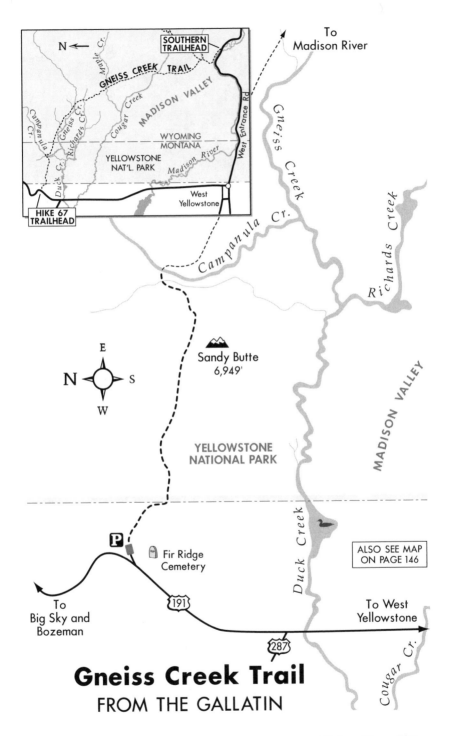

Gneiss Creek Trail
FROM THE GALLATIN

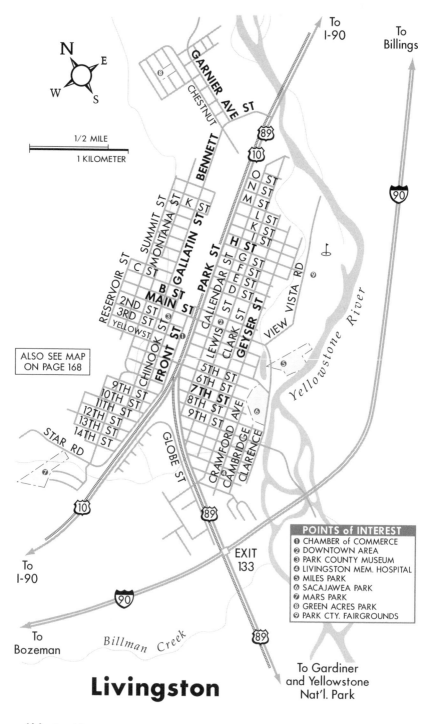

N E W S

1/2 MILE

1 KILOMETER

GARNIER AVE ST

CHESTNUT

BENNETT

To I-90

To Billings

89

10

RESERVOIR ST

SUMMIT ST

MONTANA ST

GALLATIN ST

PARK ST

SUMMIT ST
C ST
B ST
MAIN ST
2ND ST
3RD ST
YELLOW ST

K ST

H ST
G ST
F ST
E ST
D ST
ST

O ST
N ST
M ST
L ST
K ST
I ST

CALLENDAR ST

LEWIS ST
CLARK ST
GEYSER ST

VIEW VISTA RD

Yellowstone River

CHINOOK ST

FRONT ST

ALSO SEE MAP
ON PAGE 168

9TH ST
10TH ST
11TH ST
12TH ST
13TH ST
14TH ST

5TH ST
6TH ST
7TH ST
8TH ST
9TH ST

CRAWFORD AVE

CAMBRIDGE

CLARENCE

STAR RD

GLOBE ST

10

89

EXIT
133

To
I-90

90

To
Bozeman

Billman Creek

89

To Gardiner
and Yellowstone
Nat'l. Park

POINTS of INTEREST
❶ CHAMBER of COMMERCE
❷ DOWNTOWN AREA
❸ PARK COUNTY MUSEUM
❹ LIVINGSTON MEM. HOSPITAL
❺ MILES PARK
❻ SACAJAWEA PARK
❼ MARS PARK
❽ GREEN ACRES PARK
❾ PARK CTY. FAIRGROUNDS

Livingston

Paradise Valley

HIKES 68–75

map
next page

Paradise Valley is known as the Valley of the Yellowstone River. It is a wide, scenic valley bordered on the east by the steep, craggy Absaroka Range and on the west by the Gallatin Range.

Highway 89 follows the course of the river through the broad valley, connecting Livingston with Gardiner and Yellowstone National Park. Livingston sits at the head of theverdant valley in the north. The town of Gardiner is the northern entrance to Yellowstone National Park and the only approach to the park that is open all year.

The 930,584-acre Absaroka–Beartooth Wilderness, the second largest wilderness area in Montana, lies to the east of Paradise Valley. The Absaroka Range and the Beartooth Range run through the wilderness. Hikes 68–72 begin along the wilderness boundary on the east side of the Yellowstone River. The trails travel through steep, forested valleys amongst the craggy peaks of the Absaroka Range. Mill Creek (Hikes 70–72) is one of two major corridors that extend deep into the Absaroka–Beartooth Wilderness. The area is known for heavily wooded slopes and high ridge meadows. The Absarokas and the Beartooths stretch southward into Yellowstone, forming an integral part of the park's ecosystem.

The Gallatin Mountain Range separates Paradise Valley from Gallatin Canyon. The 10,000-foot Gallatin Range runs from Bozeman to Yellowstone National Park. Hikes 73–75 head westward from Paradise Valley into the Gallatins. Atop the Gallatin Divide is the 26,000-acre Gallatin Petrified Forest, an ancient forest of petrified pine, spruce, and tropical trees (Hikes 74 and 75).

For many more miles of backcountry hiking, the hikes from Paradise Valley access a vast network of trails in the Gallatins, the Absaroka–Beartooth Wilderness, and Yellowstone Park.

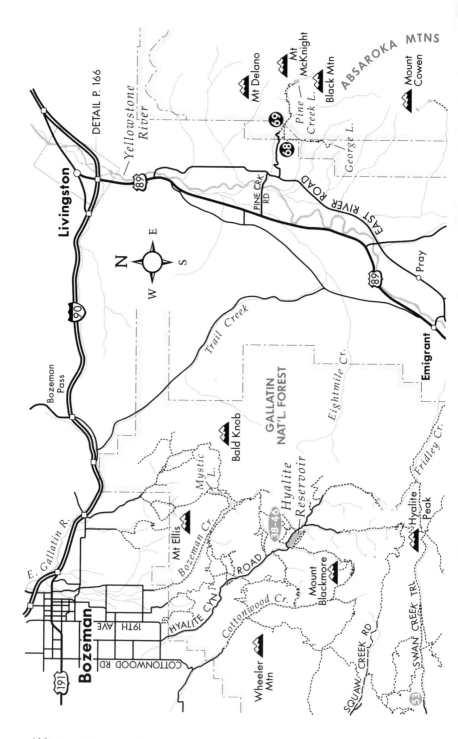

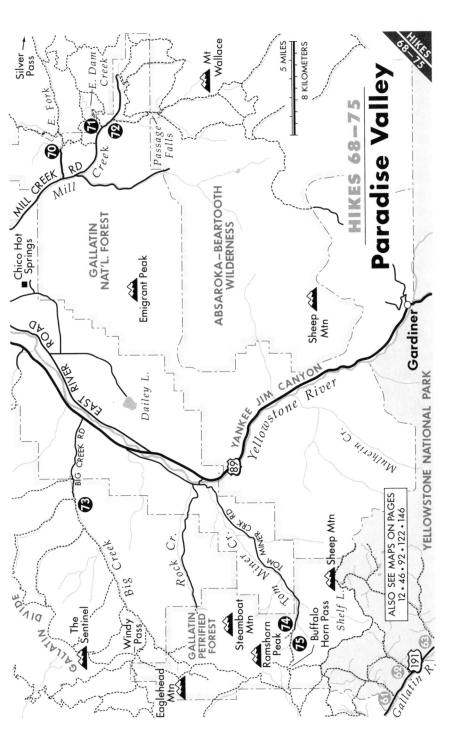

Paradise Valley

Silver → Pass

E. Fork

E. Dam Creek

71

72

70

MILL CREEK RD

Mill Creek

Mt Wallace

Passage Falls

5 MILES

8 KILOMETERS

■ Chico Hot Springs

GALLATIN NAT'L. FOREST

Emigrant Peak

ABSAROKA–BEARTOOTH WILDERNESS

Sheep Mtn

EAST RIVER ROAD

Dailey L.

YANKEE JIM CANYON

Yellowstone River

Gardiner

YELLOWSTONE NATIONAL PARK

Mulherin Cr.

BIG CREEK RD

73

89

Rock Cr.

Big Creek

The Sentinel

Windy Pass

GALLATIN DIVIDE

Eaglehead Mtn

GALLATIN PETRIFIED FOREST

Steamboat Mtn

Ramshorn Peak

TOM MINER CRK RD

Tom Miner C.C.

Buffalo Horn Pass

74

75

Sheep Mtn

Shelf L.

ALSO SEE MAPS ON PAGES
12 • 46 • 92 • 122 • 146

191

59

82

81

Gallatin R.

68. George Lake

Hiking distance: 11 miles round trip
Hiking time: 6 hours
Elevation gain: 2,500 feet
Maps: U.S.G.S. Dexter Point
U.S. Forest Service: Absaroka Beartooth Wilderness

**map
next page**

Summary of hike: George Lake (also named Shorthill Lake) sits in a depression on the lower west slope of Black Mountain. The tree-lined lake has a rocky shoreline and a towering rock wall to the east that rises 1,600 feet above the lake. The trail traverses the western slope of the Absaroka Range just outside of the Absaroka-Beartooth Wilderness, overlooking Paradise Valley, the Yellowstone River, and the east face of the Gallatin Range. En route, the trail crosses Barney Creek and Cascade Creek.

Driving directions: From Livingston at the I-90 and Highway 89 junction, drive 9.6 miles south on Highway 89 to Pine Creek Road on the left, between mile markers 43 and 44. Turn left and continue 2.4 miles (crossing over the Yellowstone River) to East River Road. Turn right and drive 0.7 miles to Luccock Park Road on the left. A sign is posted for the Pine Creek Campground. Turn left (east) and wind 2.5 miles up the foothills to the posted George Lake Trailhead on the right. Veer right on the gravel road 0.15 miles to the parking area.

Pine Creek Road is 12.3 miles north of Emigrant and 42 miles north of Gardiner.

Hiking directions: Walk up the grassy slope beneath the majestic peaks of Mount McKnight and Black Mountain. Weave through the pine forest to a posted junction at a half mile. The left fork connects with the Pine Creek Trail (Hike 68). Bear right up the mountain slope as views open of Paradise Valley, the Gallatin Range, and the Yellowstone River. Cross a trickling stream in a small grotto with ferns and moss-covered rocks at just under 2 miles. Traverse the hillside along the mountain contours, and cross a small log bridge over Barney Creek at 2.5 miles. Zigzag over a talus slope with sweeping vistas of the valley, and cross a bridge over a fern-filled drainage at 3 miles. Descend 0.6 miles into the vast Cascade Creek canyon on a series of nine rock-strewn switchbacks. At the creek, walk a short distance downstream, and rock-hop or cross downfall logs over Cascade Creek. Wind through the riparian vegetation, and ascend the south canyon slope. Leave the drainage, continuing through a lodgepole pine forest. Begin a steep half-mile climb that levels out near George Lake. The faint path is marked with a few cairns as it descends to the north shore of the lake. After enjoying a well-earned rest, return along the same path.

69. Pine Creek Falls

Hiking distance: 2.2 miles round trip
Hiking time: 1 hour
Elevation gain: 350 feet
Maps: U.S.G.S. Dexter Point
    U.S. Forest Service: Absaroka Beartooth Wilderness

map
next page

Summary of hike: Pine Creek Falls is a tall and narrow, double-tier cataract that fans out as it plunges over a large rock outcrop. The headwaters of Pine Creek form on the upper north slope of Black Mountain in the Absaroka-Beartooth Wilderness. The creek fills Pine Creek Lake as it cascades 3,000 feet down the east wall of Paradise Valley to the valley floor. The Pine Creek Trail is a 5-mile-long trail that climbs 3,100 feet to Pine Creek Lake. This hike follows the first mile of the trail along the cascading creek. The path meanders through a spruce, fir, aspen, and maple forest en route to the base of the magnificent waterfall.

Driving directions: Follow the driving directions for Hike 68 to Luccock Park Road. Turn left (east) on Luccock Park Road, and wind 3.1 miles up the foothills to the trailhead parking area at road's end (0.6 miles past the George Lake turnoff).

Hiking directions: Take the well-posted trail from the far end of the parking area. Immediately enter a deep, lush forest to a junction. Stay to the right on the Pine Creek Trail. At a quarter mile, pass a junction to the George Lake Trail (Hike 68) on the right. Cross a bridge over Pine Creek at 0.5 miles, and enter the Absaroka-Beartooth Wilderness. Continue along the north side of the cascading creek to a second bridge over Pine Creek at just over 1.1 miles. From the bridge is a dramatic view of towering Pine Creek Falls. Thirty yards beyond the bridge is a side shoot of the waterfall. Several unmaintained trails access the upper chute of the falls.

To hike farther, the trail continues to Pine Creek Lake, 4 miles ahead and 3,000 feet up. The pristine alpine lake sits in a glacial cirque high above Paradise Valley.

HIKE 68

George Lake

HIKE 69

Pine Creek Falls

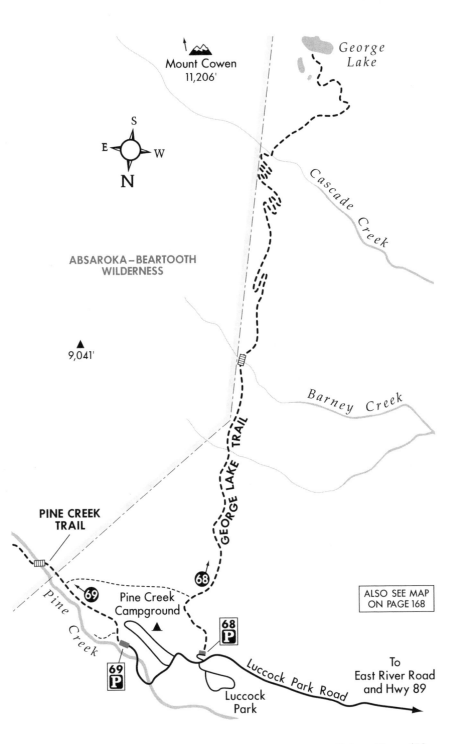

George
Lake

Mount Cowen
11,206'

Cascade Creek

S
E —⊕— W
N

ABSAROKA–BEARTOOTH
WILDERNESS

▲
9,041'

Barney Creek

GEORGE LAKE TRAIL

PINE CREEK
TRAIL

Pine Creek

69

Pine Creek
Campground
▲

68

ALSO SEE MAP
ON PAGE 168

68
P

69
P

Luccock Park Road

Luccock
Park

To
East River Road
and Hwy 89

70. East Fork Mill Creek

Hiking distance: 3 to 24 (overnight) miles round trip
Hiking time: 1.5 to 14 hours
Elevation gain: 300 to 3,900 feet
Maps: U.S.G.S. Knowles Peak and The Pyramid
  Rocky Mountain Surveys: Mt Cowen Area

Summary of hike: The East Fork of Mill Creek forms near Silver Pass, tumbling down from the upper reaches of Boulder Mountain at the Paradise Valley-Boulder River divide. The East Fork of Mill Creek Trail stretches 12 miles within the Absaroka-Beartooth Wilderness to Silver Pass on the ridge between Boulder Mountain and The Pyramid. The trail follows the creek, passing through flower-filled meadows and limestone cliffs. Atop the divide, the trail connects with the Fourmile Creek Trail and descends to the Boulder River. At the lower (west) end of the East Fork Mill Creek Trail is a connection with the Elbow Lake Trail, the main access route to 11,212-foot Mount Cowen, the highest peak in the Absaroka Range. This hike follows the lower end of the East Fork Mill Creek Trail along the watercourse and forested canyon floor.

Driving directions: From Livingston at the I-90 and Highway 89 junction, drive 15.7 miles south on Highway 89 to Mill Creek Road on the left, between mile markers 37 and 38. Turn left and continue 9.2 miles to the posted East Fork Mill Creek Road. Turn left and follow the creek 1.5 miles upstream to the posted trailhead parking area on the right.

Mill Creek Road is 6.2 miles north of Emigrant and 36 miles north of Gardiner.

Hiking directions: From the east end of the parking area, enter the dense pine forest on the posted trail. Follow the south side of the creek, skirting the Snowy Range Ranch. Traverse the hillside and loop around a small drainage to a posted trail junction at a quarter mile. The Highland Trail veers right on the east flank of Knowles Peak, connecting with the Anderson Ridge Trail and Mill Creek. Stay left, looping through a quiet side canyon and crossing a small feeder stream. Return to the main canyon with a view of bald Arrow Peak. Continue east on the cliffside path, zigzagging up four switchbacks, and enter the Absaroka-Beartooth Wilderness. Drop down and cross a wooden bridge over East Fork Mill Creek to a posted junction. The left fork follows Upper Sage Creek to Elbow Lake 6 miles ahead, at the southern foot of Mount Cowen. Stay to the right, following the north side of the creek. The trail steadily gains elevation for miles en route to Silver Pass. Choose your own turn-around spot.

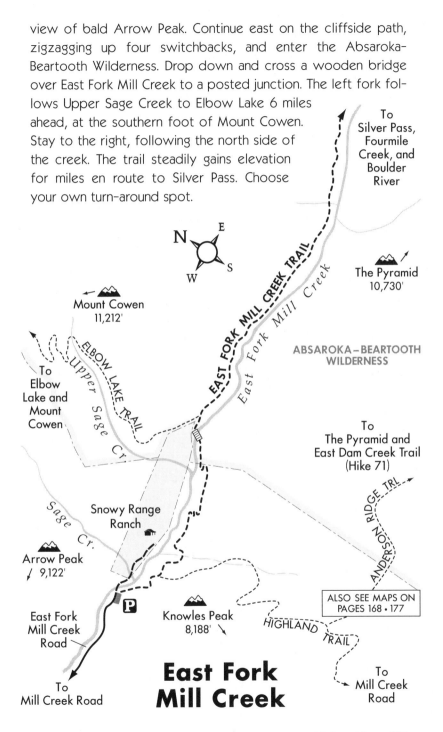

To
Silver Pass,
Fourmile
Creek, and
Boulder
River

N
E
W
S

The Pyramid
10,730'

Mount Cowen
11,212'

ABSAROKA–BEARTOOTH
WILDERNESS

ELBOW LAKE TRAIL

Upper Sage Cr.

To
Elbow
Lake and
Mount
Cowen

EAST FORK MILL CREEK TRAIL

East Fork Mill Creek

To
The Pyramid and
East Dam Creek Trail
(Hike 71)

ANDERSON RIDGE TRL.

Sage Cr.

Snowy Range
Ranch

Arrow Peak
9,122'

ALSO SEE MAPS ON
PAGES 168 • 177

East Fork
Mill Creek
Road

P

Knowles Peak
8,188'

HIGHLAND TRAIL

To
Mill Creek
Road

To
Mill Creek Road

East Fork
Mill Creek

71. East Dam Creek Trail

Hiking distance: 3 to 9 miles round trip
Hiking time: 1.5 to 6 hours
Elevation gain: 900 to 2,500 feet
Maps: U.S.G.S. Knowles Peak and The Pyramid
       Rocky Mountain Surveys: Mt Cowen Area

Summary of hike: East Dam Creek is a small tributary of Mill Creek. The creek trickles through a narrow side canyon between Mill Creek and The Pyramid. It is also a horsepacking route and cross-country ski trail. This hike follows the lower creekside portion of the trail to open meadows and overlooks. The trail makes connections with the Anderson Ridge Trail, East Fork Mill Creek, and the Moose Park Trail along the western base of The Pyramid.

Driving directions: From Livingston at the I-90 and Highway 89 junction, drive 15.7 miles south on Highway 89 to Mill Creek Road on the left, between mile markers 37 and 38. Turn left and continue 13.3 miles to the signed East Dam Creek Trailhead turnoff. Turn left and drive 100 yards to the trailhead and parking area on the right.

Mill Creek Road is 6.2 miles north of Emigrant and 36 miles north of Gardiner.

Hiking directions: Head east into the forest on a steady but easy incline. Follow the north side of East Dam Creek in the narrow canyon, passing talus slopes and small meadows. Meander through the riparian habitat with moss-covered rocks, crossing the trickling stream four times. Enter the Absaroka-Beartooth Wilderness. Continue through a lush meadow rimmed with conifers and backed by forested mountains and jagged rocky cliffs. Cross over the creek and loop around the upper end of the meadow at one mile. Traverse the hillside and curve left on a horseshoe bend. Climb to the south wall of the East Dam Creek drainage overlooking the meadow and the canyon below. Continue into a large mountain cirque and curve right, skirting the base of the upper mountains. Leave the East Dam Creek canyon, heading south. Curve along the contours of the mountain while steadily gaining elevation. Choose your own turn-around spot.

To extend the hike, the trail continues 3 more miles to the Anderson Ridge Trail, gaining an additional 1,600 feet. The Anderson Ridge Trail loops westward, joining with the Highland Trail. To the east, the trail heads up to The Pyramid.

To
Moose Park Trail
and The Pyramid

ANDERSON RIDGE TRAIL

N
E
W
S

East Dam Creek

ABSAROKA–BEARTOOTH
WILDERNESS

ALSO SEE MAPS ON
PAGES 168 • 175

To
Highland
Trail

Montanapolis
Springs

To
Hwy 89

P

Mill Creek   Road

Mill Creek

**East
Dam Creek**

72. Passage Falls

Hiking distance: 4.2 miles round trip
Hiking time: 2.5 hours
Elevation gain: 480 feet
Maps: U.S.G.S. Knowles Peak, The Pyramid, Mount Wallace
U.S.F.S. Gallatin National Forest: East Half

Summary of hike: Passage Falls is a massive, powerful waterfall that leaps over moss-covered rocks and plunges straight down to the narrow, rocky canyon floor. The waterfall is located in the Mill Creek watershed beneath Mount Wallace, just outside the Absaroka-Beartooth Wilderness in the Gallatin National Forest. The trail parallels Passage Creek on the Wallace Creek Trail. The falls is located just below the confluence of Wallace Creek and Passage Creek.

Driving directions: From Livingston at the I-90 and Highway 89 junction, drive 15.7 miles south on Highway 89 to Mill Creek Road on the left, between mile markers 37 and 38. Turn left and drive 14 miles up Mill Creek Road to the Wallace Creek trailhead parking area on the right.

Mill Creek Road is 6.2 miles north of Emigrant and 36 miles north of Gardiner.

Hiking directions: The trail begins at the bridge where Mill Creek and Passage Creek join together. Once over Mill Creek, continue south to another bridge crossing over Passage Creek. At one mile the trail crosses a stream with a small waterfall and cascade. After a second stream, the forested trail emerges into a small meadow, then ducks back into the forest canopy. At 1.6 miles the path forks just before a bridge on the left. Take the right branch to Passage Falls. Climb up the short, steep hill to a slope. From the slope are views overlooking a large meadow on private land. Take the trail to the left, and descend the eight switchbacks to Passage Falls. Return along the same route.

To extend the hike, the main trail divides at the confluence of Wallace and Passage Creek. The Passage Creek Trail follows the creek to Horse Creek and Charlie White Lake. Wallace Creek Trail follows the creek to Mount Wallace and Grizzly Creek. Both routes make connections to Gardiner and Yellowstone.

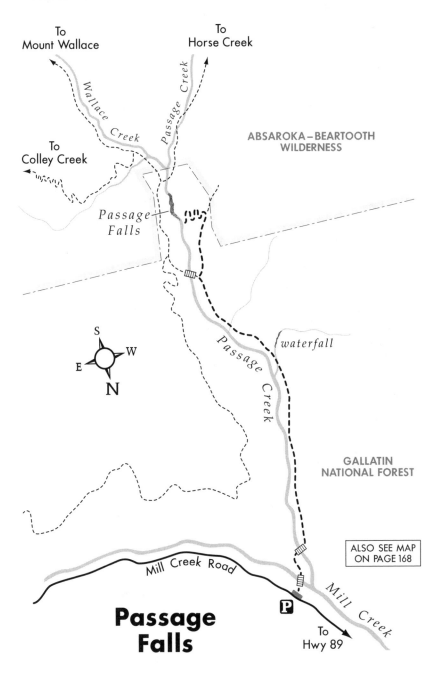

To
Mount Wallace

To
Horse Creek

Wallace Creek

Passage Creek

ABSAROKA – BEARTOOTH
WILDERNESS

To
Colley Creek

*Passage
Falls*

Passage Creek

waterfall

S
W
E
N

GALLATIN
NATIONAL FOREST

ALSO SEE MAP
ON PAGE 168

Mill Creek Road

P

Mill Creek

Passage
Falls

To
Hwy 89

73. Big Creek Trail

Hiking distance: 4 miles round trip
Hiking time: 2 hours
Elevation gain: 200 feet
Maps: U.S.G.S. Lewis Creek
       U.S.F.S. Gallatin National Forest: East Half

Summary of hike: Big Creek begins near the crest of the Gallatin Range on the east slope of Eaglehead Mountain. The creek travels more than 14 miles northeast en route to the Yellowstone River in Paradise Valley. The Big Creek Trail parallels the creek 12 miles up to Windy Pass and the Gallatin Divide Trail. This hike takes in the first two miles of the trail, passing meadows, rock cliffs, talus slides, and creekside wetlands. The trail provides eastern access to a network of trails in the Gallatin Range.

Driving directions: From Livingston at the I-90 and Highway 89 junction, drive 28.6 miles south on Highway 89 to the Big Creek Road on the right (west) between mile markers 24 and 25. Turn right and continue 4.8 miles to the trailhead parking area at the road's end. It is located across the road from Mountain Sky Guest Ranch. (At 3.5 miles is a road fork—stay to the left.)
    Big Creek Road is 6.7 miles south of Emigrant and 23 miles north of Gardiner.

Hiking directions: Head west to the bridge crossing over Big Creek, where Big Creek Road once crossed the creek. After crossing, veer right and pass a cattleguard. At 0.2 miles is a Forest Service station. Cross a second bridge and continue three hundred feet to the old trailhead information board. Climb a short hill, where the old road narrows to a footpath. The Big Creek Trail follows the forested south-facing slope. Side paths drop down to the meadows and Big Creek on the left. Slowly descend to a log bridge over Cliff Creek at 2 miles. This is the turn-around spot for a 4-mile round-trip hike.
    To continue, the trail closely follows Big Creek, crossing Cottonwood Creek in another 1.5 miles. The trail climbs to 9,200-

foot Windy Pass and the Gallatin Divide Trail on the ridge between Eaglehead Mountain and The Sentinel, 12 miles from the trailhead.

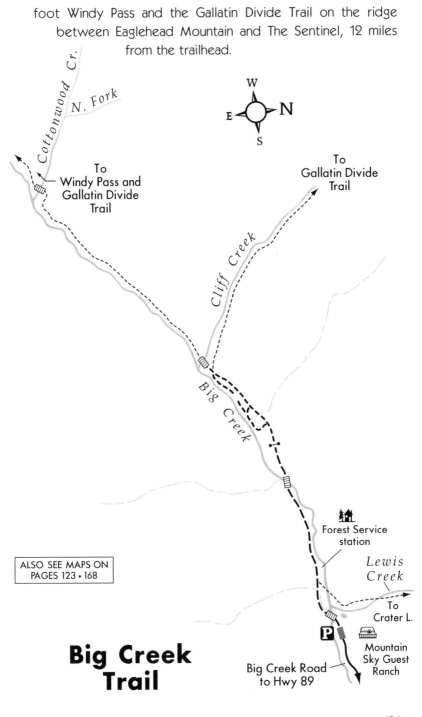

Cottonwood Cr.

N. Fork

To
Windy Pass and
Gallatin Divide
Trail

To
Gallatin Divide
Trail

Cliff Creek

Big Creek

Forest Service
station

Lewis
Creek

To
Crater L.

ALSO SEE MAPS ON
PAGES 123 • 168

P

Mountain
Sky Guest
Ranch

Big Creek Trail

Big Creek Road
to Hwy 89

74. Petrified Forest Interpretive Trail

Hiking distance: 2 miles round trip
Hiking time: 1 hour
Elevation gain: 600 feet
Maps: U.S.G.S. Ramshorn Peak
U.S.F.S. Gallatin National Forest: East Half

map
page 184

Summary of hike: The Gallatin Petrified Forest encompasses more than 40 square miles on the crest of the Gallatin Mountains. The fossilized forest extends from the northwest corner of Yellowstone National Park to Windy Pass, north of Eaglehead Mountain. The petrified trees are the result of ancient volcanic activity that buried the vast forests. The Petrified Forest Interpretive Trail begins on the lower slopes of Ramshorn Peak and Buffalo Horn Pass in Tom Miner Basin. The trail leads to a line of sculpted volcanic cliffs and caves interspersed with petrified trees and fossil remains. In one cave, a rock tree protrudes from the ceiling. From the cliffs are awesome vistas up and down the Trail Creek drainage.

Driving directions: From Livingston at the I-90 and Highway 89 junction, drive 37 miles south on Highway 89 to the signed Tom Miner Basin turnoff on the right (west), between mile markers 16 and 17. Drive 0.4 miles on Tom Miner Creek Road, crossing a bridge over the Yellowstone River to a junction. Go left, staying on Tom Miner Creek Road. At 8.1 miles, follow the campground sign, bearing left at a road fork. The B-Bar Ranch bears right. Continue on the narrow road to a road split at 11 miles. Curve right, entering the Tom Miner Campground. Drive to the upper (west) end of the campground to the signed trailhead at 11.7 miles. A campground parking fee is required.

The Tom Miner Basin turnoff is 15 miles south of Emigrant and 16 miles north of Gardiner.

Hiking directions: Head west through the trailhead gate, paralleling Trail Creek through the grassy meadow fringed with aspen and evergreen trees. At a quarter mile is a signed junction. The left fork heads west to Buffalo Horn Pass (Hike 75). Take the right fork up the meadow on the west side of a dry, rocky creekbed. Continue northwest beneath the extraordinary lava rock formations and caves. The trail leads uphill through the forest past massive lava rocks. Switchback up the south-facing mountain, passing petrified stumps to the sculpted cliffs and caves seen from below. Each cave has an interpretive station that explains the surrounding geology. After exploring the area, return along the same route.

75. Buffalo Horn Pass
FROM TOM MINER CAMPGROUND

Hiking distance: 4.6 miles round trip
Hiking time: 2.5 hours
Elevation gain: 1,450 feet
Maps: U.S.G.S. Ramshorn Peak
U.S.F.S. Gallatin National Forest: East Half

map
page 185

Summary of hike: Buffalo Horn Pass straddles the Gallatin Range Divide between the Yellowstone and Gallatin Rivers. The pass lies between the northwest corner of Yellowstone National Park and Ramshorn Peak in the 26,000-acre Gallatin Petrified Forest. Millions of years ago, volcanic mudflows smothered and preserved ancient tropical forests in this fascinating area. Exposed by erosion, petrified stumps and logs are abundant throughout the landscape. The hike begins from Tom Miner Campground and parallels Trail Creek, continuing past the creek's headwaters to a circular meadow at the 8,523-foot summit of Buffalo Horn Pass. Atop the ridge are the petrified forest and a 4-way junction, with connections to the Gallatin Canyon, Ramshorn Peak, and Yellowstone National Park.

Driving directions: Same as Hike 74.

Hiking directions: Head west through the trailhead gate, paralleling Trail Creek through the grassy meadow fringed with aspen and evergreen trees. At a quarter mile, cross a dry streambed to a signed junction with the Petrified Forest Interpretive Trail (Hike

74). Stay to the left, heading west up the sloping meadow. Traverse the edge of the hillside above the creek, alternating between shady forest and open meadows. To the east are great views of the majestic Absaroka Range. At 0.8 miles, rock-hop across Dry Creek and begin a steep quarter-mile ascent. The path remains on the north side of Trail Creek. At two miles, curve around the bowl at the Trail Creek headwaters to the meadow at Buffalo Horn Pass. At the pass is a 4-way junction, the turn-around spot for this hike.

To hike farther, the left fork heads south into Yellowstone National Park at Daly Pass (Hike 65), 2.5 miles ahead. The right fork heads 2 miles north to Ramshorn Peak. Straight ahead (west), the route descends along Buffalo Horn Creek to the Gallatin River by the 320 Guest Ranch, 7 miles from the pass.

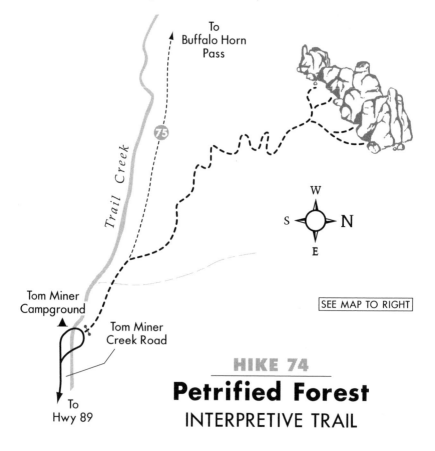

To
Buffalo Horn
Pass

Trail Creek

75

W
S — N
E

Tom Miner
Campground

Tom Miner
Creek Road

SEE MAP TO RIGHT

To
Hwy 89

HIKE 74

Petrified Forest
INTERPRETIVE TRAIL

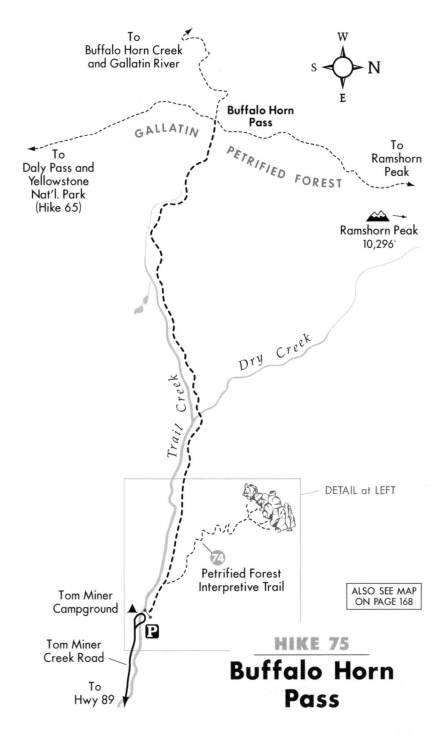

To
Buffalo Horn Creek
and Gallatin River

W
S ✦ N
E

**Buffalo Horn
Pass**

GALLATIN

PETRIFIED FOREST

To
Daly Pass and
Yellowstone
Nat'l. Park
(Hike 65)

To
Ramshorn
Peak

Ramshorn Peak
10,296'

Dry Creek

Trail Creek

DETAIL at LEFT

74

Petrified Forest
Interpretive Trail

ALSO SEE MAP
ON PAGE 168

Tom Miner
Campground

▲

P

Tom Miner
Creek Road

To
Hwy 89

HIKE 75
Buffalo Horn
Pass

DAY HIKE BOOKS

These books may be purchased at your local bookstore or outdoor shop. Or, order them direct from the distributor:

The Globe Pequot Press

246 Goose Lane • P.O. Box 480 • Guilford, CT 06437-0480
on the web: www.globe-pequot.com

800-243-0495 DIRECT **800-820-2329** FAX

Day Hikes In Yellowstone National Park

Yellowstone National Park is a magnificent area with beautiful, dramatic scenery and incredible hydro-thermal features. Within its 2.2-million acres lies some of the earth's greatest natural treasures. *Day Hikes In Yellowstone National Park* includes a thorough cross-section of 82 hikes throughout the park. Now in its fourth edition, the guide includes all of the park's most popular hikes as well as a wide assortment of secluded back-country trails. Highlights include thundering waterfalls, unusual thermal features, expansive meadows, alpine lakes, the Grand Canyon of the Yellowstone, geysers, hot springs, and 360-degrees vistas of the park.

184 pages • 82 hikes • 4th Edition 2005

Day Hikes In the Beartooth Mountains

The rugged Beartooth Mountains are Montana's highest mountain range. This beautiful range in the Rocky Mountains rises dramatically from the plains of south-eastern Montana and stretches to the northern reaches of Yellowstone National Park. Now in its fourth edition, *Day Hikes In the Beartooth Mountains* includes an exten-sive collection of hikes within this mountain range and the adjacent foothills and plains. The 87 hikes range from 11,000-foot alpine plateaus to treks along the Yellowstone River as it begins its journey through the arid plains. Includes many hikes along the Beartooth Highway and 16 new hikes in the Billings area.

208 pages • 87 hikes • 4th Edition 2006

INDEX

About the Author

Since 1991, Robert Stone has been writer, photographer, and publisher of *Day Hike Books*. He is a Los Angeles Times Best Selling Author and an award-winning author of Rocky Mountain Outdoor Writers and Photographers, the Outdoor Writers Association of California, and the Northwest Outdoor Writers Association.

Robert has hiked every trail in the *Day Hike Book* series. With 23 hiking guides in the series, many in their third and fourth editions, he has hiked thousands of miles of trails throughout the western United States and Hawaii. When Robert is not hiking, he researches, writes, and maps the hikes before returning to the trails. He spends summers in the Rocky Mountains of Montana and winters on the California Central Coast.